Naomi B. Levine, JD

For 25 years, Naomi Levine was Senior Vice President for External Affairs at New York University (NYU). In this capacity, Mrs. Levine was responsible for development and fundraising; press and public relations; alumni relations; and all special events relating to and involving alumni, trustees and donors. In 1978 when Mrs. Levine came to NYU, the University was close to bankruptcy – raising only between $20-30 million a year, which included funds for its medical center, hospital and law school. Under Naomi Levine's direction, and with the help of an extraordinary Chairman of the Board, Board of Trustees, and several very involved Presidents, NYU began to raise $400-500 million a year and has become a great global center of learning.

Following her tenure as Senior Vice President of NYU, Mrs. Levine was Special Advisor to the President of New York University; Founder, Chair and Executive Director of the NYU George H. Heyman, Jr. Center for Philanthropy and Fundraising; and Chair of the Boards of the NYU Edgar M. Bronfman Center for Jewish Student Life and the NYU Taub Center for Israel Studies. She also became a faculty member in the NYU School of Professional Studies teaching *Ethics, Laws and Board Governance of Nonprofits.* Naomi Levine serves as a member of the Committee on Character and Fitness of the New York Supreme Court. She is also a Board member of Jonas Nursing and Veterans Healthcare and she works closely with the NYU Rory Meyers College of Nursing, which is an area of special interest to her.

On October 27, 2005 Naomi Levine received the NYU *Presidential Medal* signed by three Presidents, which is the highest honor the University confers. On May 22, 2013 she was awarded an honorary *Doctor of Humane Letters* from Hebrew Union College. On May 18, 2015 she received a special *Humanitarian Award* from the NYU College of Nursing. And on June 5, 2017 Naomi Levine received the *Maimonides Award* from Hillel International for her service to the Jewish community.

Prior to NYU, Mrs. Levine was the National Executive Director of the American Jewish Congress, a national organization concerned with the political, social and economic needs of Jews in the United States and the security of people in Israel and the Diaspora. She was the first woman to hold a position as executive director of a major Jewish organization that had within it men and women. For many years she was Assistant Professor in Race Relations at John Jay College of Criminal Justice.

Naomi Levine is at the present time a consultant to the MorseLife Foundation in West Palm Beach, Florida. She is a lawyer, a graduate of Columbia Law School (1948), where she was an editor of its *Law Review*. She is expert in constitutional law as it relates to civil rights, civil liberties, church-state separation, discrimination and the rights of minorities.

Before her work with America Jewish Congress, Mrs. Levine practiced law in New York City. She received her undergraduate education at Hunter College (1944) and is the author of several books and articles on intergroup relations. She is also the author of the book "Politics, Religion and Love," a scholarly biography of Edwin Montagu, Secretary of State to India, 1917-1918 -- a man who played an important role in the history of England before and during World War I.

May 2019

From Bankruptcy
To Billions

Fundraising the Naomi Levine Way

16 Simple Rules for effective fundraising
without charts, pyramids, consultants and feasibility studies.

by Naomi B. Levine

New York University

The Presidential Medal
Naomi Levine

For over a quarter century, you have brought your exceptional talents to bear on the world's largest private university. With discipline and energy, passion and wisdom, you have touched and transformed this institution. Highly revered by your colleagues as Senior Vice President for External Affairs, you led them in the first billion-dollar fundraising campaign by any American university, which you completed and then repeated—all in record time—giving shape to the NYU we see before us today: a vibrant, world-class center of teaching and research thriving in the heart of New York City. The results of your efforts are everywhere to be seen on our campus: the Edgar M. Bronfman Center for Jewish Student Life, the Skirball Department of Hebrew and Judaic Studies, the Taub Center for Israel Studies, the Silver Center, Trustee Row, Tisch Hospital, the Helen and Martin Kimmel Center for University Life, the Tisch School of the Arts, the Leonard N. Stern School of Business, the Steinhardt School of Education, and the Robert F. Wagner Graduate School of Public Service. Moreover, through a gift that literally goes on giving, you established the Center for Philanthropy and Fundraising in the School of Continuing and Professional Studies to teach the principles of your profession and to enhance its stature. Lawyer, advocate, author, philanthropist, orator, raconteur extraordinaire, you are a glorious inspiration to all who seek to live lives of purpose, infused with intellect and guided by noble intention. On the 27th day of October, 2005, therefore, we take great pleasure in exercising the singular privilege of presenting you, Naomi Levine—with the deep appreciation of three presidents and the enduring gratitude of our entire community—New York University's Presidential Medal.

John Brademas	L. Jay Oliva	John Sexton
President	President	President
1981-1991	1991-2002	2002-

Table of Contents

Introduction – A Primer

As I sit down to write this book I feel a little embarrassed because I have, in the past, ridiculed the multitude of books on fundraising which are published each year. I have found most of them duplicative, adding little to the material already on hand. They all seem to say the same thing – devoid of new ideas or innovative approaches, often using new jargon for old ideas.

My students, however, pointed something out to me that I had not thought about and which prompted this book to be written. They taught me, something that I think I taught them, that effective fundraising is a reflection of the personalities involved and as a result there is no duplication in these books, as every fundraiser is different. Every fundraiser brings to their fundraising their own persona, how they think, how they develop relationships, how they sell their product, how they feel about their product, and why they believe their product is unique and deserves support. In that spirit, I do have something to say. For my approach to fundraising is a reflection of who I am and how I relate to people, my values and my life experience.

There is another reason that, I believe, justifies this book. For 26 years I was a Senior Vice President of New York University and the chief professional who led its Billion Dollar Campaign. (It was the first Billion Dollar Campaign of any university in the country.) During this period I saw the University move from close to bankruptcy to become one of the world's great global institutions of higher education.

At one point in the 1970's, NYU had funds sufficient only for a three month operation and a debt of $40 million. The situation was so bad that the clerical staff and faculty were asked to voluntarily take a cut in their salaries. Competition from other colleges and universities was severe, especially with the announcement of open enrollment by the City University of New York.

Academic standards were modest. Many alumni were bitter and disillusioned when the University sold its beloved Heights campus in 1973. Fundraising was dismal. During these years the University raised between $20 million and $30 million a year, which included its Medical Center (school and hospital) and its Law School. The school had few if any dormitories. It was a commuter school, with most of its students taking the subway to school every day and living at home. Students from outside New York City were few. There was no recreation center and no central library, with books scattered throughout the University in areas that were often airless and badly lit. NYU was not a university of "first choice" for students or faculty.

Today, just 35 years later, New York University is not only fiscally stable, but is recognized as one of the world's most acclaimed centers of higher education and research. Students are clamoring to come to NYU. Its academic rankings are among the highest. It is raising more than $400 million a year and it completed one of the largest - if not the largest - building campaigns in the last decade, which included the construction of a magnificent sports center, a beautiful new student center, six new dormitories, and scores of new laboratories and classrooms.

What produced this miracle? How could a near bankrupt university become a great university with a balanced budget, more applications than it can handle, distinguished faculty, and outstanding fundraising in so short a time? It is that story as a "case study" that this book analyzes. Hopefully, the lessons and processes explained in this case study and the critical role that fundraising played in New York University's transformation will be useful to other organizations, both large and small, which face problems similar to what NYU faced 25 years ago.

SO LET ME REPEAT: LARGE OR SMALL, THE PROCESS DISCUSSED IN THIS BOOK AND THE RULES SET FORTH ARE GENERIC, I BELIEVE, AND ARE FUNDAMENTAL TO ANY EFFECTIVE FUNDRAISING CAMPAIGN.

So this book does two things. First, it will describe the rules and process of fundraising as I see it through the prism of my own personality. And second, it will tell the NYU story – "the last academic train out of the station." It is a truly remarkable story that demonstrates that in addition to the personalities involved in effective fundraising, there is a process and rules that can turn a mediocre fundraising program into a highly successful one. The NYU story is told here because it is a dramatic example of how the rules set forth here transformed this University and can do the same, I believe, for any nonprofit.

This book summarizes those Rules. They are not complicated. Their implementation is the hard part. It is in the implementation that the "art," not the "science," of fundraising comes into play. It is in the implementation of the rules that the personalities of the fundraisers, their ability to relate and develop relationships, their creativity, their verbal and written skills, and their passion for their organization become key factors. But the best fundraising personality – without knowledge and understanding of the Rules – will not be effective. It is in that spirit that the Rules set forth on the following pages are presented.

History

As a starter, let me underscore again that this is a book about fundraising – not about New York University. I begin, however, with the history of NYU during its fiscal crisis merely to underscore the fact that whether you are a large or small organization – a university or a soup kitchen – you can face excruciating problems, financial and otherwise, that can often spell the demise of your organization. Size does not guarantee survival, nor does it determine success.

Before trying to understand how NYU remade itself, it is useful to look at its history during the 1960's and 1970's. Indeed, as you look at the enormity of the challenges that the University faced in those years, its stunning recovery and growth seems even more remarkable.

First, like most universities throughout the country, NYU during the 1960's had its share of student unrest on campus. This frequently disrupted classes and caused faculty and the administration to spend more time on how to deal with these outbreaks and less time on educational policy. I have no doubt that these disruptions were partly to blame for the decline in student applications to the University during this period, but for NYU there were other problems. The decline in the quality of life in New York City, especially in the Greenwich Village area; the increase in drug sales and crime; and the intense competition for recruitment by the City University of New York (CUNY) with its open enrollment announcement – all of these played important roles in lessening the interest of students to come to NYU and the Greenwich Village area.

So, by the 1970's, New York University was facing impending financial disaster. The crisis, in fact, was so bad that the prospect of bankruptcy was a very real possibility. President James Hester and the Board of Trustees then made the wrenching decision to sell its much loved University Heights campus. This campus in the Bronx was beautiful. It had magnificent buildings, dormitories, athletic fields, and one of the country's most elegant libraries, Gould Hall, designed by Stanford White. The Bronx campus also housed the Undergraduate College of Arts and Science. According to Chancellor McCracken, who devised the idea and began its construction in 1892, stated:

"The Heights would be where students could enjoy the country environment, and yet be able to study close at hand the great city."[1].

But, President Hester had no alternative but to sell. If he did not sell, it was clear that the University would have to close. That he faced tremendous opposition from students, faculty, and alumni, goes without saying. They were outraged, angry, and bitter. They loved the Heights. With its sale many felt their ties to the University were broken. These feelings were so strong that it took several years to overcome. But, as said above, Hester had no choice. The money received from that sale gave the University some breathing room. It paid off its $40 million debt to creditors and it provided help for salaries and scholarships.

But even that money was not enough to keep the University from moving closer and closer to bankruptcy. Financial conditions went from bad to worse. In 1975 a new President, Dr. John Sawhill, was brought in to try to salvage the situation.

President John Sawhill

John Sawhill was not an academic. He was an economist, a PhD graduate from NYU's Stern School of Business, and had a career history in both corporate financial services and management and in government as the Director of the Federal Energy Administration. Sometimes if you face severe financial difficulties it is wise to bring in a CEO or president who has a strong background in finance – someone not afraid to cut costs, cut staff, and even cut programs where necessary. Sawhill was such a man.

To achieve the balance in the budget, he was relentless in cutting costs, in avoiding duplication academically and administratively, consolidating departments where necessary, and, most importantly, in pressing for the sale of the C.F. Mueller Company, a pasta factory that NYU's Law School had received through a trust fund. The Law School Foundation acquired this company in 1947 and the income gave the Law School the financial strength, unlike the other schools within the University, to become one of the country's leading law schools. Sawhill argued that the Law School would not be viewed as a first-rate school if the University went bankrupt. Martin Lipton, then Chair of the Law School Board and now the Chair of NYU's Board of Trustees, not only agreed

---

[1] Dim & Cricco, *The Miracle on Washington Square* (Lexington Books, 2000) (pg. 113)

with this but took the lead in pushing this forward and urging that a portion of the cash that would be gained by its sale be used to help the University as well as the Law School. How the money would be divided between the University and the School of Law was hotly debated. Mr. Lipton played a key role in resolving that conflict. The result was that the money was divided between the University and the Law School. The argument that the Law School would have very little chance of becoming a leading school of law if the University closed won the day.

Still, despite the Mueller sale, the wrenching cost cutting, and the firing of scores of people, the financial health of the University remained precarious. It became clear to Sawhill that the only way to really save the University was through fundraising. Until that time fundraising was minimal. The Board did not view fundraising as a priority and faculty and deans were only minimally involved in raising funds from private sources. Sawhill, on the other hand, viewed fundraising as a critical responsibility of the Board and the entire University – faculty, deans, and administration. He developed, together with the fundraising staff, the 16 Rules set forth on the pages that follow. They became the epicenter of the University's fundraising efforts.

Rule 1
Fundraising: Everyone's Job

If you find yourself in an organization with a Board that shares the view that fundraising is not a priority and is the responsibility only of its fundraising staff – you are in trouble. Sawhill, unlike his Board, knew that fundraising had to become a major matter of the deepest concern for the whole University (or any nonprofit), including its President, its Chairman, its Board, its Deans, and its Faculty, if it was to survive. Fundraising cannot be left only to the development staff. It cannot be assigned only to a staff of fundraisers. It must be viewed as central and pivotal to the organization's life. It must be viewed as a priority of every component within the institution. Many times executive directors of nonprofit organizations, including presidents of universities, believe that if they have a strong development staff they can distance themselves from the fundraising effort. If the leadership of your organization thinks this way – your fundraising efforts are doomed. Every unit in your organization must be involved or you cannot succeed.

Many organizations view their fundraisers, moreover, as the least important component in their organization. As a result, fundraisers are not always treated with professional respect and do not receive the salaries they deserve. No organization can treat their fundraisers in this fashion and be successful in its efforts to raise money. There are 1.5 million nonprofit organizations in the United States today. They raised in 2017 $410.02 billion. In achieving that remarkable goal, fundraisers played a key role.

It must be kept in mind, too, that without a flourishing nonprofit sector, our country would not be what it is today. The $400 billion that nonprofits raised helped the country build great universities, hospitals, performing and visual arts centers and provide services and care for the sick, the aged, the poor and hundreds of others who need help. The 82,516 foundations with assets of $855.8 billion made grants of $50 billion. Clearly, our country benefits in remarkable ways by these grants and other funds raised by philanthropic donors.

More people work for nonprofit organizations than work for the State and Federal governments combined. Furthermore, one nonprofit, i.e., Harvard University, has an endowment that is larger than the GNP of several African nations.

Nonprofits have built our private universities, our hospitals, libraries, research institutions, museums, opera companies and other performing arts companies, while at the same time building homes for the homeless, the aged and the blind, and providing soup kitchens and the social services that our country desperately needs.

Those nonprofits have provided jobs and investments in physical and human capital, while supporting new research and training which in turn improves our entire economy, indeed, our entire society. In her book *The Greater Good* (a "must" reading for anyone interested in the philosophy of American philanthropy), Claire Gaudiani makes another point worth projecting when talking about fundraising. She states:

> Most people think that Americans are generous because we are rich. The truth is that we are rich, in significant part, because we are generous. It is not surprising that Americans know so little about the economic impact of citizen generosity in the country's growth. We tend to see giving as something that is just *good* and *nice* to do, which it is. We do not, unfortunately, recognize it as a major contributing factor in our economic, social, and political achievements as a nation.

> Fifty-one percent of all hospital beds are funded by citizen generosity. Forty-nine percent of all two- and four-year institutions of higher learning are not-for-profit. Citizen generosity funds a little more than 20 percent of all students in institutions of higher learning, 95 percent of all orchestras, and 60 percent of social service organizations. (Fleishman, "Philanthropic Leadership.") In 1997, non-for-profit organizations spent $700 billion in cash. That's cash. It does not include volunteered time. And it's about 8 percent of the economy. Generosity is not a luxury in this country. It is a cultural norm, a defining characteristic of our successful economy and our reasonably successful society.[2]

---

[2] Gaudiani, Claire, *The Greater Good How Philanthropy Drives the American Economy and Can Save Capitalism*, Chapter 1 (Times Books: Henry Holt and Company, LLC., 2003) (pgs. 9-10)

We need not belabor the point. Clearly, the nonprofit sector is a critical component of our society. WITHOUT THE FUNDRAISERS, THE NONPROFIT ORGANIZATIONS WOULD HAVE DIFFICULTY SURVIVING. IT IS THIS PHILOSOPHY, I.E., THE IMPORTANCE OF FUNDRAISING AND OF THE FUNDRAISERS THAT MUST BE PROJECTED TO EVERYONE WITHIN YOUR ORGANIZATION.

At NYU, and I suspect at many nonprofits, the Board and the University as a whole was not respectful of its fundraisers and did not have a culture of giving. The two factors are usually different sides of the same coin. Both sides must change if an organization wants to survive and grow.

Fundraisers must be adequately paid. The Board must understand their importance. Special seminars must be held for the Board about fundraising and especially about the critical role fundraisers play in the fundraising efforts of any organization. It might be useful to invite a philanthropist to such a meeting to discuss how a fundraiser helped in his or her philanthropy. On pages 7-8, the role of the professional fundraiser is discussed in greater detail.

Rule 2
The Role of the CEO, President or Director

The CEO, president or director* must set the tone for making fundraising an organization's priority. At NYU this is precisely what John Sawhill did. He increased salaries for the development staff. He put the office of Senior Vice President for External Affairs next to his. He would meet with the Senior Vice President and other development staff throughout to go over the week's fundraising activities. He insisted that the development staff arrange at least a minimum of 4-5 fundraising meetings a week for him – not an easy task. He constantly stated that "good fundraising is not achieved by postage stamps, but by shoe leather."

*From now on I will use the title director in place of CEO or president, except when referring to the existing presidents of universities.

In this he meant that only meetings and more meetings and more meetings could identify donors. Only in this way could he tell the NYU story and begin the cultivation of donors – a prerequisite to effective fundraising. "This is why," he said, "the process is called <u>development – not fundraising</u>." He made this clear at every opportunity.

He was a very difficult and hard taskmaster. It was not easy to work with him, but the staff had great respect for his drive and commitment to fundraising and we knew his approach was correct. Whatever pressure he put on us, he put on himself too. He never stopped and he spent probably more than one third of his time in fundraising, but he felt that only in that way would he be able to save the University. In short, he set the tone within the NYU academic community concerning fundraising. He made it clear that he would be the principal salesman, that he would make calls himself, but that he expected to get help from every unit within the University.

This intense presidential involvement in fundraising was carried on by his successors Dr. John Brademas, Dr. L. Jay Oliva, and Dr. John Sexton. All of them spent more than one-third of their time raising funds.

John Sawhill also explained repeatedly that when people give a gift they want to meet the head of the organization, the person who is running the organization, and the person who is going to care for their money. That is why he, as President, had to play so intimate a role. People who give money want to meet the director. They want to be sure that they can trust him or her and that their money will be spent well. That was his basic philosophy. That was what he preached at every opportunity he had.

He also made clear to the faculty and deans that he could not raise money in a vacuum. They had to give him ideas. They had to be concerned with fundraising in the same way that he was. Faculty, therefore, were encouraged to come up with ideas that he could then package and promote. Faculty, understanding the dire needs of the University, were only too glad to help. And their efforts were rewarded in the saving of the University.

With this rule as your guide, make certain that in your organization your program staff, financial officers, and volunteers are part of your campaign. They must be kept up to date on your progress and their input must always be sought.

Because the director of any organization must be the organization's key fundraiser, make certain that the director you choose has experience in raising funds, or at least has the personality for relating to people, and has the ability to understand the mission of the organization in-depth and the role he or she must play in its life. The director must feel passionate about the organization and be able to verbalize those feelings. He or she must also understand that they will have to allocate a major portion of their time to fundraising as the director – perhaps as much as 50 percent. This is true whether he/she has or does not have a first-rate development office.

I cannot stress enough the importance of personality. Always keep in mind that fundraising is called "development" precisely because it depends on developing relations with people. A director who begrudgingly does fundraising, whose distaste for it shows clearly on his or her face and in his or her demeanor, will not be able to develop relationships with potential donors. A prerequisite in the choice of a director is someone who likes people as much as they like the mission of their organization. "Liking people" and "relating to them" is difficult to teach.

Sometimes directors, after a few successful calls and after meeting some extraordinary people in their search for donors, become more comfortable with fundraising and develop an increasing interest in people. Many potential donors, especially those who started out with little financial support but with intelligence and creativity created a new business or expanding an existing one, are fascinating people. The reluctant fundraiser finds that developing relationships with such people is a pleasure, not a chore. With this transformation, the reluctant director becomes a champion fundraiser.

Keep in mind that a director's responsibilities in fundraising does not stop with the solicitation of a gift. The development process requires constant stewardship. This entails keeping in touch with donors after they have made their gift through dinners, luncheons, phone calls, emails, letters, site visits, and always keeping them apprised on how the organization is doing – and especially how the project the donor funded is being implemented. Accountability and disclosure for donors is absolutely essential.

Rule 3
An Effective Chairman of the Board of Trustees Absolutely Essential

Sawhill recognized, too, that he could not do fundraising alone, even with the help of a well-run development office. He required a Chairman of the Board committed to fundraising and for whom fundraising was a priority. His first step, therefore, on assuming the Presidency, was to find someone who would chair the Board, who would work with him closely in fundraising, and would have contacts within the city of New York that could help with finding prospective donors.

Finding an effective Chairman is probably one of the most important function of any organization's board. In this search, the director must play an important role. He or she usually serves on the search committee and does some initial screening for this committee. This applies whether the organization is a large one or a small one.

The Chairman is absolutely critical. The director and the board should not rush in their task of finding one. They should be prepared to spend a good deal of time in this search. Sawhill followed that rule. He took his time and he chose very wisely. The person he recommended as the new Chairman of the Board was Laurence Tisch, who was Co-Chair and CEO of Loews Corporation and CEO of CAN Financial Services. His companies owned real estate, hotels, movies, insurance, Bulova Watch Co., and Lorillard Tobacco. He graduated from NYU in 1942. Mr. Tisch also had been involved in many philanthropic ventures in the City. He was highly respected, a very successful businessman, a generous philanthropist, and someone who understood the dynamics involved in an effective fundraising campaign. He knew the New York City philanthropic community and it, in turn, knew and admired him.

Not every organization can find a Larry Tisch, but they should be able to find someone who is respected and liked in their own community. This person must, of course, be concerned with social issues, believe in your organization, and have the time to be actively involved. A chairman must also be someone who knows other people in the community who might be willing to join the organization involved. And perhaps most important, the chairman must be someone who can make some financial gift to the organization. He cannot ask other people to make gifts if he does not set an example.

There are often local banks and local businesses in a community where the CEO of that bank or business feels it important to be involved in the community. This is good business and gives the local business needed visibility. If such a person becomes chairman of the board of a local nonprofit organization, it is a valuable contribution to the visibility of that company and often results in more business. In searching for a chairman, therefore, do not overlook the businesses in your community, including small businesses and stores that also need the community's good will.

Once you find a chairman, you must be careful to respect the time limitations that might face a chairman. Keep in mind that chairmen are volunteers and they have professional and personal responsibilities. Assure a potential chairman that you will be very careful about how you use their time. Report to him regularly, but this does not necessarily mean meeting after meeting. Use emails, memos, phone calls, etc. and when you are setting up meetings, be sure to find dates and times that are convenient for the chairman.

A director of a nonprofit, or the director of any company, serves the chairman and must always keep that in mind. In preparing an agenda for a meeting, for example, discuss it first with the chairman. Send him drafts of the proposed agenda and always consult with him. And if he must make a report to the board, prepare draft remarks for him. In other words, try to relieve him of some of his responsibilities so the job of chairman is not a chore.

And if and when press releases go out, try to have them released in the chairman's name so he can receive some outside visibility and some credit for the organization's achievements. Egos exist on every level, so always try to pay tribute to your chairman's contributions and find the time to thank him both publicly and privately.

Here I end with a comment I made at the beginning of this section: a chairman is indispensable to an effective campaign. Your choice of a chairman and your relationship to that chairman is critical to the success of your organization and your ability to carry on in your role as director. If you do not relate well to your chairman, you are in trouble. So help your board in the choice of a chairman. Define your relationship early in his tenure and make every effort to service him properly – always retaining your own dignity and importance.

It is very hard to "define a relationship." So much depends on the personalities that are involved. I know I may be repeating myself when I underscore the fact that the chairman is a "volunteer" who is giving his time and efforts not for a salary, but because of his commitment to the organization. He has his own professional and personal life that is surely his priority.

The director or development must make it easy for him to carry out his chairmanship and at the same time his personal life. Draft letters and reports for him, making sure he knows they are drafts that he can change or revise. Find out when it is the best time to call him. Find out if he prefers email or letters and use the format he prefers. Be sure to hold meetings with him in a place that is comfortable for him. Give him your ideas, making clear that they are "just suggestions" and his opinion is critical. Do not raise issues with him, like politics and religion, about which you know he does not agree with you. If you do disagree with him on an issue, tell him "you are not sure what approach is best" and you will take it to the president, director, or another trustee to get another opinion. Give him visibility and let the board know of what he is doing. Be sure by your behavior that he will respect you. Remember also that he plays a critical role in your hiring and firing.

I'll end here like I started: relationships depend on personalities. All I can do here is to give you some general advice, but the rest is up to you.

RULE 4
The Board of Trustees: A Key Role in Fundraising

The Board of Trustees is the governing body of every nonprofit. It is responsible for overseeing the financial and program activities of the organization and for making certain that its mission is being carried out properly. It has both the fiduciary duty for the proper administration of the organization and is also legally and ethically liable for its activities.

The concept of fiduciary duty is a basic principle in law. It demands of the board members that they act in the best interest of the organization. The fiduciary responsibility demands that the board members carry out their duties with care, loyalty, and obedience.

"On performing duties, a board member has to perform his or her duties in good faith; with care an ordinarily prudent person in a like position would exercise under similar circumstances and in a manner the director reasonably believes to be in the best interest of the mission, goals and purposes of the corporation."[3]

In addition, board members must play a key role in fundraising. Larry Tisch and John Sawhill at New York University recognized this as soon as they took over their respective responsibilities. In one voice they made clear to the board that they expected board members not merely to sit on the board because board membership was an honor and privilege. They expected that board members recognized their serious responsibilities. They must attend meetings. They must

---

[3] (Pg. 15, Sarbanes-Oxley for Non-Profit Boards, Peggy M. Jackson, John Wiley & Sons Inc (2006) quoting from A White Paper prepared by the staff of Charles Grassley, former Chairman, Senate Finance Committee, after hearings on fiscal and government abuses and diminished public trust in nonprofits.)

serve on committees. They must participate in budget and audit discussions and in decisions involving the programmatic and academic mission of the University and they would be expected to <u>give</u> money, help <u>get</u> money, or – to put it crassly, <u>get</u> off the board. These are the 3-G's of board responsibility.

Obviously, just being able to fulfill these functions and to make a gift were not the sole requirements of sitting on the board. Board members have to be persons concerned with social issues, both broadly and those specific to your organization, such as higher education in NYU's case. In addition, the community had to view them as decent and honest people. This standard is applicable not merely to colleges and universities, but to every nonprofit. Your board must symbolize what your organization stands for. Its members must be respected in the community. Board members give the organization its aura of importance and respectability. This must always be a consideration when choosing a member of the board.

Let me here raise a question that is discussed in greater detail under Rule 16, Ethics in Fundraising. Do you take money from someone accused of unethical behavior? Recently a trustee who has given a great deal of money to NYU was accused of sexual misconduct. His money has helped students with scholarships, paid for extraordinary faculty, and helped build dormitories.

My answer, and the answer of the NYU Board, was "No." We do not take money from anyone accused of unethical behavior. We are a university. We must set an example to our students and must act as we hope they will act – ethically. But be sure that before you make such a decision that the case has been examined thoroughly. Do not accept gossip. If the matter is being investigated legally, be sure you wait for a court decision. And, above all else, make sure that the board agrees with you.

On a related note, it is an axiom in fundraising that "people give to people." Donors are more likely to give to someone they know, some peer, somebody involved in their lives in some fashion, somebody whom they respect. Again, that makes the role of the Trustees so important. They know prospective donors. They must open the doors for the president or the chairman to meet them. They have to be prepared to go out with the president, the chairman or the director of development on such calls. Over and over again, Mr. Tisch and John Sawhill reiterated their mantra: no organization large or small can afford to have people on the board who are not ready to give money and help raise it.

Some members of the NYU Board accepted this new "culture of giving." Some left the board and new members were added. The new members consisted of presidents of major banks, important leaders in the financial and insurance worlds, and many men and women involved in the real estate industry and in the professions. These are the principal "industries" of New York City, and from which NYU would raise its financial support. It was, probably, the most impressive board in the city of New York when completed. It continues today to be that kind of board.

Committees

An effective board works through committees and each board member should be required to serve on at least one committee. The committees generally consist of at least an executive committee, an audit and budget committee, a program committee, and a fundraising committee. Other committees are often created to meet the special needs of each organization. An executive committee usually consists of the director, chairman of the board, chairman of the audit and budget committees, the organization's chief financial officer, the chairman of the program committee, and the chairman of the fundraising committee. This committee carries on the business of the organization between meetings of its Board of Trustees.

A fundraising committee consists of a small group of trustees who are responsible for the overall fundraising efforts of the organization. It is an absolute essential in any fundraising effort. The fundraising committee must meet frequently to review and suggest prospects, take special assignments, and generally give advisement and direction to the professional staff. At New York University, George Heyman, managing director of the now defunct Lehman Brothers with a distinguished career in finance and philanthropy, was chosen to head the Trustee Development Committee. Between meetings, he and the fundraising staff kept the Board of Trustees informed by phone, emails, memos and meetings about success stories, failures, new prospects and dollars received.

Volunteers

Having a small group of volunteers who are assigned the special task or working exclusively on development is an important component in any campaign. It provides, moreover, another vehicle for volunteers, which are very important in the functioning of an organization – and especially important in fundraising. Every study shows that people who volunteer generally give more money than those who do not. In addition, working in development gives the volunteers something to do. Most volunteers complain that they are not used effectively by their organizations. They attend meetings and sometimes make a gift. For most people those are not satisfactory functions; they want more.

Fundraising is an answer to that problem. It provides many important functions for volunteers, including working on special events, phonathons, fundraising dinners and luncheons, finding new donors, making calls, writing letters, and participating in stewardship. Many organizations have special training sessions for volunteers, especially for those involved in fundraising. Keep in mind that nearly half of the American population volunteers. This is a unique feature of American society. A good campaign never loses sight of their importance.

Importance of Professional Staff

As important as volunteers are, few organizations have been able to survive without a professional staff. Fundraising has become far more sophisticated in recent years. It is no longer just "selling cookies for the Girl Scouts." It requires special knowledge in planned giving, soliciting major gifts, the psychology of fundraising, using technology for research and stewardship, direct mail, phonathons and an understanding of Federal and State laws and the ethical issues involved. Today our world has become far more complex and the need for trained professionals who understand the intricacies of the philanthropic world and how to influence giving has never been greater.

In a volatile and global economy every cultural, educational and nonprofit organization is at risk of losing funds even from what were once reliable sources. As government agencies experience budget cutbacks and foundations earn lower interest on investments, revenue that is typically dedicated to gifts – grant-making organizations in both the public and private sectors are becoming more focused and sophisticated in choosing where they give. All of these require more professional knowledge than in the past.

It is for that reason that courses and degrees in fundraising and grant-making are now being offered by colleges, universities and fundraising associations. Indeed, in some institutions Master's degrees are being offered in recognition of the complexity of this field and the importance of educated professionals.

If you are in a position to do so, urge your development staff to take some of the courses offered. While taking a course does not guarantee that a fundraiser will be a great fundraiser, it certainly will give them a better understanding of the intricacies of fundraising and how they could best fit into this profession. Writing courses, for example, will never make an ordinary person into a Hemingway, but it can help a student write better. The same principle applies to fundraising. You may never become the "Hemingway of fundraising," but you will have the advantage of knowledge drawn from the expertise of others which will add immeasurably to your own effectiveness as a fundraiser.

Volunteer leadership must respect and recognize the knowledge a professional fundraiser brings to the job. That respect is shown by attitude and by salaries. The attitude of volunteers to professionals is very difficult to define. It is often suggested that this is best achieved by stating in writing the functions of each. I am not sure this is the answer. It simplifies a very complex relationship. While it helps to have some benchmarks on the functions of each, relationships – like love and friendship – are hard to pigeonhole. Every relationship is different. The most that I can recommend is that professionals must recognize they cannot do their job without volunteers. And volunteers must recognize that they need professionals. They must view each other as partners and recognize the role that each can play. Professionals cannot be arrogant about their knowledge. And volunteers must recognize the special gifts that professionals bring to the field. Discussion, compromise and respect is all that we can expect in any partnership relationship.

Let me underscore here that the job of the fundraiser is a very difficult one. With more than 1.5 million nonprofits needing money to survive, it is not easy to get the philanthropic gifts that nonprofits need to exist. For that reason, development staff leave their positions frequently. The tensions are very high. This is sad, because the longer the fundraiser stays with an organization the more knowledge they have of the organization, its commitments, and its leadership. What can we do about this?

I believe it is the job of the director to understand the tensions that the job creates and be prepared to help the fundraiser by ensuring both financial and operational support as needed. The director should meet with fundraisers on staff often and, of course, pay him well. Look at fundraising as a group activity where everyone helps. There is no gift that only one person gets. Someone makes the appointments, does the research, and writes the proposals. Every fundraiser is part of a group, which makes his job easier. As I said before, talk with him frequently, help him in difficult situations, go with him on calls when appropriate, praise him when a gift comes in, and, wherever possible, try to help solve the problems that he faces.

RULE 5
Development Office Staff: Centralized, Well Paid, Respected

At New York University John Sawhill paid a great deal of attention to the development staff – how it was organized and how it was paid. He found that the University had many different schools and units with their own fundraising staff (like many other nonprofits), with each unit acting as if they were independent organizations. The development staff, moreover, was basically underpaid and badly organized.

The first thing he did was develop a <u>centralized</u> fundraising operation. There was one goal for the entire University, with each school having to raise a specific portion of that goal. Each of the school's fundraising staff was <u>hired, fired, and supervised by the Senior Vice President who reported to the President</u>. Salaries were increased and new, more desirable space was found for them so that their image immediately heightened within the University family.

The Senior Vice President in charge of development was given special status and attention with, as said earlier in this book, offices right next to the President. Fundraising was now viewed as an important component in the University family. Even with this centralization, however, each dean was expected to be part of the team and play an important role in the fundraising of their school. The "team spirit" was constantly discussed. Deans generally were involved in raising smaller gifts, $500,000 or less, plus alumni cultivation. The larger gifts were usually assigned to the President or a Trustee.

The Senior Vice President was to act as a "clearing house" regarding donors, and to coordinate the schools' solicitations so that duplication in requests was avoided. If a Dean wanted to visit Mr. Smith, for example, but another school had been cultivating Mr. Smith in the past, it was the job of the Senior Vice President to act as the referee to decide which school had priority, and if he or she sensed a conflict, the President, who was the final arbitrator, was consulted.

This centralized approach can be applied to any large organization, not merely a university. Like a university, many organizations have chapters and different units within their institution. In such situations, I recommend a centralized operation with a single goal divided among its various parts. As explained above, centralization minimizes duplication. Most important, there has to be one person in charge of the entire campaign who, like in the NYU situation, acts as a referee and a conduit to the president and to the chairman of the board who act as the final arbiter.

The Development Office

The organization of the development office at NYU was simple. I believe, its general lines of responsibilities are applicable to all organizations.

A Senior Vice President for External Affairs, whose portfolio included fundraising and alumni affairs, was in charge of the development office. The staff included:

- The Director of Development who supervised the entire staff, also serviced the Senior Vice President and George Heyman and the Trustee Development Committee. The Director had one major gift officer working with him. Both reported directly to the Senior Vice President.

- Each School had a school Development Director, plus anywhere from one to ten other development staff. Law and Medicine had the largest number of staff, as they had the largest goals. The other Schools either shared a development officer or had, at most, 2-3 development officers.

- One person was hired for coordinating the work with foundations and one person to do the same for corporations.

- One person was assigned to planned giving.

- One person was responsible for special events and had one assistant.

- Two people were assigned to the "Annual Campaign" and to work closely with each School. This group coordinated direct mail solicitations and phonathons.

- Several people were hired to work on alumni relations.

- Several people were assigned to a Research Center where a special computer system was established to track gifts, do research on possible donors, and enabled donor stewardship.

- Three writers were also on staff to help write "thank you" letters and proposals. In addition, every development staff was expected to write their own "thank you" letters and draft proposals, etc.

- There was a support staff of about ten secretaries.

It was, by today's standards, a very small staff. As the fundraising grew year by year, the staff was increased modestly. It never was very large.

RULE 6
Choose Development People Who Are Interesting Human Beings

While education and experience are important in choosing development staff, the development staff at NYU was supposed to have, in addition, an entrepreneurial spirit, be creative, able to write, speak, and relate to people. Regardless of the position they held within the development office, staff had to be "interesting well-read people" so that donors would enjoy talking and relating to them for fundraising is not primarily "asking people for money." That is part of it, but not all. It is the <u>cultivation of people</u>. It is developing relationships. Here is where the "art," not the science, comes in. Here is where your personality and how you relate to people is key. Every situation is different, as different as every donor, and fundraisers need to be adaptable.

By adulthood much of a person's personality is set, but there are ways to change it, to improve. Of course, read the *Chronicle of Philanthropy* and other books and magazines on development and philanthropy, but, more importantly, read *The New York Times*, *The Wall Street Journal*, *The Economist*, *The New Yorker* and other magazines. Read books and join organizations. Become a whole person. Be interested in the society in which you live. Show that you are interested in current issues in politics, education, healthcare, the environment, women's rights, etc. This makes it possible to cultivate a donor by discussing areas of his or her interest. When Larry Tisch was involved with CBS, the staff who related to him were asked to read everything that the press was reporting about CBS. Why were people critical of Mr. Tisch? What was happening in his news division? Why is *Murphy Brown* a success? What happened to *Murder She Wrote*? Development staff was urged to read those articles so that they could talk with Mr. Tisch in the area of his greatest interest. Developing a relationship starts with such conversations.

RULE 7
Understand Why People Give

Everyone involved in fundraising should understand why people give. The reasons are many and often complex.

- **Altruism:** Many people give because they believe in a cause that they hope will make the world better.

- **Give Back:** The desire to repay an organization, typically a school or hospital, is a strong motivation for giving. For example, hospital campaigns are often based on "grateful patients" who want to give something back to the doctor who helped them. Alumni campaigns also depend on this emotion.

- **Who Asks:** People are prone to give to people they know, trust, and respect. It is harder to say "no" to a friend or business associate than to a stranger. For that reason it is important to choose wisely as to who will join you on a call. "People to People" is not merely a catch phrase, but a valuable bit of advice.

- **To Be Part of a Social Group:** In every community there is usually a special social group or groups that people want to be part of. Sometimes it represents the "socially and economically elite," i.e. the New York Metropolitan Opera or the Metropolitan Museum of Art in New York City. People will frequently give a donation just to be seen with this group. It's "the place to be." Other people find a sense of belonging when they are part of a group and make this gift to be assured of their place in this group.

- **Tax Benefits:** American tax laws are generous in providing tax benefits for charitable gifts. Although such benefits may be a factor in making gifts, it is not the most important one. Moreover, many large gifts were given to charities long before the tax code added its tax incentives. (The Rockefeller and Carnegie gifts are just two examples.)

- **Being Asked:** Do not underestimate the importance of "asking." Many times people do not give simply because no one asked. And never be ashamed of asking. You are asking for a good cause – not for yourself. Keep in mind also that people are often flattered that they are asked.

- **Feel Good:** Strange as it may seem many people just "feel good" when they make a gift. There is a warm, often indescribable feeling of pleasure when one can help another person or a cause.

- **Self Interest:** Some people give because they believe there is a benefit, whether professionally, socially, or otherwise, in giving the gift. This is especially true of corporations.

- **Religious Commitment:** All major religions include a mandate to care for the poor, the aged, the ill, and to help "your brothers in need." All studies show that religious affiliation influences giving.

RULE 8
Be Able to Verbalize the Uniqueness of Your Product

While John Sawhill was recruiting a new Chairman and new Board members, he was also working with appropriate staff and faculty to define what was special and unique about NYU. As said before, there are more than 1.5 million nonprofits in the United States today. Why should donors give to NYU? Why is NYU special? Why is it unique? These are basic questions that every organization must ask itself when it begins a fundraising campaign.

NYU started from the assumption that its biggest competitors were the CUNY open enrollment colleges and Columbia University. As for the CUNY schools, NYU decided that it had to distinguish itself dramatically from those universities. It had to cut back on its size, raise its SAT requirements and overall academic standards, consolidate its operation on Washington Square, build its College of Arts and Science, use its fundraising to attract distinguished faculty, and present itself not as a "last resort university" or an open enrollment university (which was open to everyone), but rather as an academically demanding university that would recruit top students and top faculty. More than half of the money raised in its opening campaign was devoted to attracting new faculty and in providing scholarships for students.

In regards to Columbia University, NYU distinguished itself in a very special fashion. It described Columbia as a school with a wall around it, divorced from New York City; a special enclave of privilege in upper Manhattan. NYU on the other hand had no wall around it. It was part and parcel of the City of New York. It would become a "private university in the public service." Every one of our schools was asked to develop programs with New York City institutions. For example, our School of Education developed scores of programs with the public schools of the City. Our Law School developed programs to handle the legal problems of the poor in the City. Our Medical School developed an increasing number of programs with Bellevue. Our Dental School sent out vans to nursing homes in the City to treat the aged who had dental problems. Our Tisch School of the Arts developed very close relations with the theaters in the City. Our Stern School of Business developed programs together with Wall Street and the financial world. So when you attended NYU you not only received an education academically, but you were also exposed to the real world – to New York City, with its myriad of institutions, businesses, professionals, and the performing and visual arts. Thus, New York City would become the campus of NYU!

As part of its transformation, NYU decided to do extensive recruitment outside of New York City. No longer would it be a "subway school" (like the CUNY colleges). Instead it would be a national and international university. This required using some of the money that was raised to be used not only for scholarships and faculty, but also for building dormitories and other facilities for a "living on campus" experience. (Very little was put in the endowment, as the trustees decided first to "build" the University and only when that was completed, to set aside funds for endowment.) Seven new residencies were built, offering modern suites with kitchens, living rooms, cable TV, and internet connections. One of the most impressive dormitories was the Palladium building, which houses more than 900 students, encompasses a 65,000 square foot athletic and recreation facility that includes a pool for swimming, diving, and water polo, a basketball court, and exercise spaces.

In addition, a new sports center was built, providing facilities for basketball, tennis, swimming, fencing, volleyball, and dance. A new student center, with extensive facilities for student clubs was built. It is a signature building on Washington Square and holds a 1,022 seat state-of-the-art theater – the largest theater south of 42nd Street and the only performing arts center south of Lincoln Center. Its projection booth and integrated audio equipment enables it to hold film screenings and film festivals, including the Tisch School of the Arts' "first run" film festival and the bi-annual NYU International Student Film Festival. As a result, our connections with Broadway expanded and NYU is now the number one university in the country for study in the performing arts and filmmaking studies.

All of these facilities, which cost more than $1 billion, plus the new classrooms and laboratories, gave a new face to the University. More than approximately 11,000 students now live on campus. We are dramatically different from the CUNY colleges and our deep involvement with New York City differentiates us dramatically from Columbia University. It has given us a unique face - something that has been critical in our fundraising.

So whether you are a university, a large organization or a small one, it is a basic rule of effective fundraising that you try to present your "product" in a way that makes it unique and special. May I suggest you not only write out your Mission Statement but also use it in any and all brochures you produce, and be sure you understand the statement and can verbalize it, as well as write about it. As you think about this, keep in mind that people like to give to new ideas – to ideas that will help make the world a better place.

RULE 9

Capital Campaign: Know What It Is and When to Embark On It

The principal components of a capital campaign are: it is <u>intense</u>; it runs for a <u>specific period of time</u>; and it raises money for a <u>specific purpose or purposes</u>. Following the NYU model, you do not begin a capital campaign until you have first established fundraising as a priority in our organization. In addition, you must also have a good chairman in place, a board ready to help in fundraising, and a good development staff. Furthermore, your organization should have already received some major gifts from some of your trustees and other potential donors and have developed a large enough donor base of possible future donors that would assure the success of the campaign. You also must make certain before you go public that you know what your priorities are.

Only when New York University had all of those components in place did John Sawhill announce a capital campaign in 1976. The campaign would be for three years and attempt to raise $111 million dollars. The goals were: to increase scholarship funds; to continue its extensive recruitment of top faculty; and to move ahead with its building program.

Building an endowment was not part of the goals of this campaign. The trustees were very clear in stating that first the University must regain its position as a major educational institution. The University had to put the money raised in to paying its debts, getting top students and top faculty, and continuing to build the facilities to accommodate those groups.

The campaign, as I said above, was for three years. That meant that only $37 million would have to be raised each year. Since the University was already raising close to $30 million annually at the time, setting a $37 million goal was not exorbitant. The importance was that it was the first campaign the University had launched in a long time. People understood the need for it. The fear of bankruptcy was still hanging over the University and getting private money remained a high priority.

One word about setting goals: do not set them too high. It is better to be modest and surpass your goal than to set a goal that you cannot reach. Once the goals were set and everything else was in place, the University held a luncheon at a hotel in the city to make its announcement. Its lead gifts were reported. Special praise was given to those who gave the initial gifts to help start the campaign. The President and Chairman of the Board spoke. It had the aura of an exciting event. The press covered it and the University was off with flying colors to the first of its many campaigns. Such capital campaigns provide special opportunity for new brochures, for providing medals and citations for major donors, and provide many opportunities for the use of volunteers.

At the end of three years, NYU surpassed its goal and was prepared in 1982 to announce another campaign – this one to raise "a million a week for 100 weeks." That was a catchy phrase that caught the attention not only of the potential donors and trustees, but of the press. Actually, when translated into yearly figures the "one million a week" meant the University would have to raise $52 million a year. That was not an exorbitant number, as we had proved that we were able to raise $35-37 million in each of the preceding three years. Again, we were cautious in setting our goal. We knew what we could raise. We were not extravagant in choosing a million a week for two years. But the idea of raising that much money each week was a very exciting vision and it helped generate a sense of importance, urgency, and excitement within the University.

The "One-Million a Week for 100 Weeks Campaign" was again a huge success. The University raised $110 million by 1984 and in 1985 it then felt confident enough to announce a "One-Billion Dollar" capital campaign to be raised in fifteen years. It was one of the first universities in the country to set a goal of one billion dollars. That meant that the University would now have to raise $70 million a year. Again, keep in mind that that was not an exorbitant amount, since we already proved we could raise $52 million a year. But the "One-Billion Dollar" number attracted the press (something all capital campaigns aim for) and it excited the leadership by the audacity of the number "one-billion." This campaign, too, was successful, raising its goal in ten years, not fifteen.

It was during this capital campaign that the University created the Sir Harold Acton Society. All donors who contributed $1 million dollars or more got a beautiful Sir Harold Acton Medal at a black-tie dinner. To this day, once a year the University holds a Sir Harold Acton Gala Dinner. It serves as an incentive for million dollar and over gifts and it added an exciting tone to the campaign. Capital campaigns lend themselves to the creation of such special awards and recognition. Donors enjoy such recognition and deserve it. Be creative and devise as many of such opportunities as you can.

RULE 10
Process in Place

Now we come to the most difficult part of a fundraising campaign, i.e., to develop a process that will bring in a maximum number of donors.

Each year approximately 83% of the money raised by NYU comes from gifts of $1 million or more. This is not unique to NYU. It is true of any major campaign. In 2017, of the $410.02 billion raised by nonprofits, $70 billion came from individuals and $35.70 billion (or 9%) came from bequests. Added together this shows that all told, 79% came from individuals, 16%, or $66.90 billion, came from foundations, and $20.77 billion, or 5%, came from corporations. These numbers underscore the importance of individual gifts. Many were very large gifts.

UNFORTUNATELY, THE WEALTH OF THE COUNTRY IS IN THE HANDS OF A VERY SMALL PERCENTAGE OF OUR POPULATION. Most small nonprofit organizations in our country do not have access to these people, but there are enough people with sizable incomes that should be capable of making large gifts to your organization. The secret is finding them and finding some program within your organization that interests them. (See Rule 15 Technology for a discussion of research and how this should help you in finding prospects.)

What a large or major gift is will depend very much on the size and budget of the organization involved. It could be as small as $500 and as large as $10 million or more, but whatever the size of the major gift, it is critical to any campaign, large or small. (In Rule 11 on Annual Campaigns we discuss other aspects of fundraising. In this section on process we will concentrate on major gifts through individual solicitations.)

Now back to the process. While many organizations may develop modifications of this process, I am listing below the steps that NYU took and takes in developing its campaign.

1) The President of the University, having made fundraising an all-university priority and having the Chairman in place, plus a Board understanding its fundraising responsibilities, now begins the campaign by asking the Chairman of the Board for a gift.

2) After the Chairman has made a gift, which should be viewed as a "lead" gift, he and the President should choose a few potential donors among the trustees, who they felt were capable of a large gift and with whom they had good working relationships. They then visited those trustees, all of whom made their gifts of $1 million or more to start the campaign. Remember: your major gifts may be much smaller. But the principle remains: all of your trustees must be visited personally and all should make some gift.

3) After these preliminary gifts were made, a note went out to every trustee telling them that a campaign was beginning. No public announcement would be made until we had visited every trustee and some potential donors so that we had some idea of how much money we could expect in the campaign.

4) After this letter went out, the Senior Vice President in charge of development, the President, the Chairman of the Board, and sometimes other Trustees visited every single other trustee. In most cases they were not asked for money at this time. Instead, they were told about the campaign and what the University's needs were. They were asked if they would give us a list of any friends or potential donors who we could put in our database.

We also asked them if they would "help us" with a gift in the campaign. We were deliberately vague at this point, merely trying to discover whether they would be prepared to make some gift once the campaign began. In some cases an "ask" was made, but this depended on individual circumstances.

5) After this visit, the development staff began to work together with the research center. Other names were collected from our alumni lists, donor lists, etc., and a huge database was put together that would be the foundation of our campaign.

6) The university then had some idea of what its potential fundraising goals could be. Some organizations hire consultants to do this – a feasibility study. NYU never did that. It believed that its staff was capable of putting this together. The University was not prepared to pay $100,000 or more that consultants charge for this study. Moreover, if our own staff was

involved in assembling the database, they would have a better feel for the potential that the University had in raising its funds.

Most fundraising books also suggest that consultants not only prepare a feasibility study, but suggest that the organization design a pyramid which indicates how many million dollar gifts, for example, must be achieved if the campaign is to be successful. How many gifts between $500,000 and $1 million need to be solicited, etc., down to the smaller gifts at the bottom of the pyramid. I never saw much sense to designing a pyramid. My feeling was that I need as many large gifts as possible. If I got two million dollar gifts or five million dollar gifts, then the entire pyramid would be changed. So why prepare it at all? But I guess that habits are so ingrained in any profession that reason is not sufficient to change it.

Another word about consultants. If your organization can afford it, I always believed it was better to have fundraisers in house instead of using consultants. People on staff, working only for you, bring a commitment to, and knowledge about your organization that consultants, who work for several organizations rarely can provide. There are, of course, exceptions, but that was my experience.

In addition, consultants generally come in and tell you what the rules are. They tell you what you need to find a good chairman and a good board. But then the task is yours. You have to find the chairman! You must find the board members! They do not bring a list of potential donors. You must compile the list.

Sometimes there are consultants who do stay with an organization a long time and do get involved in implementation, but that is rare. On the other hand, if your organization cannot afford its own fundraising staff, then of course a consultant can help. But it is not my first choice.

7) As stated above, we started with our trustees. We found out everything we could about them: their ability to give; what their interests were; and what charitable gifts they had recently made. The people in research were indispensable in collecting this information. We then brought these names to our Trustee Development Committee.

8) We went over these names with the Trustee Development Committee not only to get their opinion about the prospects, but to get their comments about who should be meeting with each of the prospects, assuming we were planning to go further with them. For example, if the person was in real estate, we would discuss what real estate person should meet with him. If he was in insurance or finance, we would think of people who we

felt were his peers and someone that he would respect. During the twenty years that Larry Tisch was Chairman, he joined most of these meetings, as did the President and Senior Vice President for External Affairs. They had as many as four or five meetings a week until every trustee was personally visited.

9) After we identified the person who we thought might want to support a particular project and identified the person who should be the one to go to the first meeting, the staff in development usually called that potential donor on behalf of Mr. Tisch and the President and asked for an appointment. We usually explained on the phone that we wanted to bring the person up to date on NYU and ask their advice on something in which the University was interested. If, for example, we were going to meet a man interested in investments, we made certain to comment about our investment policy, explaining on the phone when we were asking for a meeting that we hoped he could help us as we explored this area. In soliciting major gifts, meetings are essential. You do not raise this kind of money with letters. Only one-on-one meetings can begin the development process. So, keep in mind: you do not raise money with "postage stamps" but rather, through "shoe leather."

10) We usually had our meetings at breakfast. This was convenient for the businessmen. (At that time, and this shall be commented on later, we did not have as many women on our prospect list as we would have today.) At these breakfasts we did not say: "We are glad to meet you and could you give us money?" We never did that. At those meetings we talked about their interests, a little about the world, areas of mutual interests and then, if appropriate, we would ask his advice on some University policy. We would then discuss particular programs at the University in which we thought they might be interested. We listened and let the prospect talk, so that we would discover their special interests. Listening is key. Let the prospect talk so you have a better idea of what might be of interest to him. Then we asked whether they would have any time to take a tour of the University, have lunch with the President, and get a better sense of what we were doing. We tried to get a date at breakfast for such a follow up meeting. If they accepted our request for a visit, we knew they were interested.

11) When they came down to Washington Square to meet with the President, an appropriate Dean, and faculty from areas in which we thought they might be interested, we took them to visit those departments. At this luncheon with the President and Dean we also tried to involve them

46

in something. If there was going to be a concert or film festival at the Tisch School of the Arts, we would invite them to that. If there was a seminar at the Law School, we would invite them to that. If we had an advisory committee on filmmaking we would, if appropriate, invite them to sit on that committee. The purpose of these meetings was to try to <u>involve</u> them in some aspect of University activity. Involvement is key. It is the most effective way of developing a relationship. Every organization should try to have their donors visit their offices. Seeing a program at work is worth a hundred words.

12)   We did not rush to ask for money. The quicker you ask, the less money you will receive. We were very careful to develop a relationship with the prospective donor before we would ask for money. The name of this effort is "development." It is the key to success.

13)   Once we received the commitments of the trustees, we continued the process we used with our trustees: finding new prospects through research and suggestions from our trustees; doing our homework on each prospect; holding breakfasts and lunches, etc.; and cultivating each prospective donor and involving them in some fashion in the University. It is a slow process. There are no shortcuts.

14)   While this is going on, the President was meeting with each Dean to determine their needs. When we had a respectable amount of money in hand or pledged and had a good idea of what was needed in the University, a proposed goal and plan for the campaign was brought to the Board of Trustees. Once they approved it, we then went public.

15)   Our public announcement usually came at a luncheon. The President and Chairman of the Board would speak; goals were set; the lead gifts were announced; and a campaign committee was created. This was usually the Trustee Development Committee with a few additional trustees and donors added.

We made the announcement as exciting as we could, trying to find something in our goals that would interest the media. For example, if some of the money would be used for some research in malaria, we would feature it. If we planned a new dormitory, we would have photographs, etc. In short, announcing a campaign is as much or more a PR event as a fundraising event.

16)   In designing your campaign and your lists of prospective donors, do not forget the women. They not only should be on your board, but they should be intimately involved in the committees of your organization.

Women today own more than 51% of the nation's wealth. They own the majority of all stocks traded on the New York Stock Exchange. Many have inherited their wealth (women live 7-10 years longer than men) and many are now earning very good salaries. Many have important positions in law firms, in the medical profession, and on Wall Street.

Should fundraisers have a different approach when they are soliciting women than when they are soliciting men? There is no unanimity about this. My own experience has been that there are not many fundamental differences. (The differences are usually age and economic status – not gender.) But more research is clearly needed. I believe that when you have a good product and you sell it with passion and commitment and you know the woman is interested in such projects, and the right person has come to meet with her, there are no gender differences in the way that you sell your product.

17) Be certain in your campaign to pay attention to planned giving. One-third of gifts made by individuals come through wills, charitable lead trusts, pooled income, etc. This is a very important area and no campaign should be without someone in charge of this. That person should be a lawyer. In addition to the person assigned to planned giving, every member of the staff should know about this area. They should take courses, read books devoted to planned giving, and be able to at least begin preliminary conversations about these instruments with potential donors. Usually the staff person does not have to go into great detail. It is appropriate for him to say: "If you are interested in this as a method of giving a gift, may I suggest that you talk with your lawyer and your accountant." That is probably the best way to go, but knowledge about planned giving is critical.

18) In putting together a database and planning your campaign, using the Internet and technology is absolutely essential. The research people now have at their disposal technological systems that segment people. They have research tools that can give them a tremendous amount of information, including Hoovers.com, Edgar.com, the Foundation Center, Guidestar.org, and Grantsmart.org. Your staff should also read *The New York Times, Forbes, Business Week, The Economist* and *The Wall Street Journal*, and other publications that relate to business. You can get a good deal of information from these sources, as well as the many other sources that are online today.

19)   Never forget stewardship – caring for the donor <u>after</u> he makes a gift. A donor who has already made a gift is your best prospect for future gifts. Keep him or her informed on what is happening with the project he has funded. Regularly send them information about your organization and remember birthdays or special times in the donor's life and constantly think of ways to keep the donor involved. Accountability and disclosure are keywords you must never forget. And for major donors, always find the time for a visit and a phone call.

RULE 11
Do Not Forget Your Annual Campaign

So far in this case study we have concentrated on major gifts and "one-on-one" solicitations, but no campaign should ever forget or ignore the smaller gifts that one can count on year after year in response to an annual campaign drive. These gifts are important because they are usually unrestricted, which is very important for an organization to have, and because from their ranks often come future larger gifts. Annual appeals usually involve direct mail, i.e., appeal letters, followed by telephone calls (phonathon or a telemarketing company) and if research shows that the annual gift a donor makes indicates a potential for a larger gift, then meetings and cultivation follow.

Usually current donors who gave in the last appeal are written to first. Donors who gave previously but not yet in this campaign and persons who never gave but have some relationship to the organization are also sent solicitation letters as the campaign unfolds. The secret of direct mail is, of course, the letter and even the envelope. It must tell the organization's story in an exciting way. It cannot be too long. It must look like a personal appeal. Even the design of the envelope is important, as the appeal can be effective only if the letter is opened.

It is a difficult piece to write and many times requires special help. Organizations have become more sophisticated these days by segmenting their lists by age, occupation, gender, location, etc., in order to better tailor their direct mail appeals. This should be done whenever possible.

The phone calls that follow can be made by a telemarketing company or by volunteers or by both. NYU has always used paid NYU students to make these calls. There is something especially appealing when students make the calls, but working with students and volunteers is often difficult. They need more training and are not always reliable. For that reason many nonprofit organizations use a telemarketing company. Their professionals need less training and are more sophisticated callers who generally always show up, but they do not have the special appeal that the volunteer and/or the student has. I think every organization must examine this themselves and decide which is more effective for them. Sometimes a combination of both is the best.

Be certain that in negotiations with your telemarketing company you are clear about how much money the company keeps and how much money they return to you. Some companies keep as much as 75%! The Better Business Bureau suggests no more than 35%.

Annual appeals should not stop during a capital campaign. Donors should be told early in the campaign the need for the unrestricted annual gift and why their gift to the capital campaign should be viewed as "over and above" their annual gift. While this is the general wisdom often given on this subject, it is often more complicated. To some it might seem in bad taste to ask a donor who just gave a million dollar gift to the capital campaign to give another $1,000 to the annual fund. The donor might feel he is being "nickeled and dimed." In other cases he would understand the difference between the two campaigns and be quite willing to make this added donation. In short, each donor should be treated individually and no blanket rule should apply. Here timing is most important, too. Try not to make your direct mail appeal at the same time a donor is being visited for a major gift. Again, each donor must be handled separately.

In discussing donors, a question is frequently asked as to whether there are any significant differences between "old" and "new" philanthropists. The media frequently makes this distinction, attributing to the "new" philanthropists a desire to be a genuine part of the projects they support; to know how their money is spent; and to support innovation. I believe, and my article develops this, that these distinctions are not correct; that the old guard was equally concerned about the creative use of their money; and their desire to be involved in the organization they support is as strong as the "new philanthropists."

RULE 12
Special Events: Part of a Fundraising Campaign

The number and type of special events are limitless and can include luncheons, dinners, galas, golf and tennis outings, theater parties, auctions, fashion shows, etc. It was the opinion of the staff of New York University that most special events, especially dinners and galas, were not cost effective and in many cases did not raise large sums of money. For example, if an organization sold 500 tickets at $1,000 each, it would gross $500,000. In today's market it would cost at least $250,000 for the food, venue, flowers, liquor, invitations, programs, etc., netting only $250,000. The latter figure, moreover, does not include staff time in making hundreds of calls to get 500 people to buy tickets. In addition, the details of any dinner or gala are tremendous and also require a great deal of staff time. If, however, the event is used as a way of soliciting gifts prior to the dinner, or if the dinner is sponsored by an organization or person, then it might be viewed as worth the amount of time, effort and costs involved.

There is another reason for having dinners and other special events. Dinners have a potentially valuable public relations component. If the program and the speakers are well chosen then the chance of getting an item in the press is very real. Many organizations use their dinners and galas for that kind of public visibility. Galas also bring in new people. If you are going to honor someone, he or she will unquestionably bring in their friends and that gives you additional names for your database. So do not get me wrong, there are advantages in holding such special events, but I do not view them as a way of raising a great deal of money. I view them more as a public relations event, getting more visibility and bringing in some new people for future development and cultivation.

Public Relations

Do not underestimate the importance of public relations. Media coverage and other public relations techniques not only for dinners, but for all aspects of organizational work is an important prerequisite to any effective campaign. Your organization's work, its contributions to the community, and its leadership must be known before people will make a gift.

Every effort must be made to get your stories to the press, radio or television. Do not concentrate on *The New York Times* or *The Wall Street Journal*. Local press and local radio stations are eager for stories. Cultivate members of the press as you would prospects. Send them invitations to events. Send them ideas you may have about a possible story. Send them material about the programs you are involved in. If new or interesting members join your board, try to get stories about them or profiles in the newspapers. Write your press releases carefully because many press officers are so busy that they will use a press release exactly the way it is sent to them. If your release is well written, this encourages them to use your release.

Your annual report and any program materials should be widely distributed. The story headlined in *The New York Times* shown below did more for the reputation of New York University than any fundraising activity we could have ever conceived.

Buying Excellence: How N.Y.U. Rebuilt Itself -- A special report; A Decade and $1 Billion Put N.Y.U. With the Elite

By WILLIAM H. HONAN

Ten years ago, New York University was what college-bound students from New York regarded as a safety school, fourth or fifth on their application lists. If you didn't get into Cornell or Brandeis or Brown University, you could always commute to N.Y.U.

But the administration, doing some long-range planning, decided that being the safety school was not good enough. So in 1984, it began a brash campaign aimed at moving the school into the nation's top tier of universities. And according to academics around the country who have looked on with envy, the strategy worked.

In what was a remarkable fund drive at the time, the university set out to raise $1 billion. But unlike most institutions, which plow such sums into their endowments and then live off the interest, N.Y.U. spent nearly all of it to rebuild the university.

It lured scholars from Princeton and Harvard and Stanford and Chicago. It created a top neural science center. It opened a new performing arts school, an institute of mathematics, an Italian studies center.

It raised the average Scholastic Assessment Test score of entering students from about 1100 five years ago to over 1200, making it one of the more selective schools in the country. It built new dormitories to attract students nationwide: 10 years ago, 18 percent were from outside New York City; today, 73 percent are. And it has increasingly become the first choice of students who apply.

Continue reading the main story

"They have simply made enormous progress in the last decade," said Harold T. Shapiro, the president of Princeton University, who served as chairman of the evaluating team for N.Y.U.'s reaccreditation last year. "In several areas, they're every bit as good as the best."

Joel Conarroe, president of the John Simon Guggenheim Memorial Foundation, which evaluates faculty at colleges nationwide for its prestigious fellowships, said, "N.Y.U. has recently become a great university, and if it continues to develop at this pace, it may well gain admittance early in the next century to that small, charmed circle of exceptionally distinguished institutions."

The story of how the university came to inspire wealthy benefactors to help upgrade it into what is now very nearly the Greenwich Village equivalent of Columbia uptown, commanding tuition, fees and room and board of $26,800 and attracting students of nearly equal caliber, involves alumni like Laurence A. Tisch, the head of CBS, who fanned out across the city in the last decade to woo rich friends and acquaintances for investment in the transformation.

It involves administrators like John Brademas, the former N.Y.U. president who used the money to convert a collection of blighted and crumbling buildings into a modern urban campus and who tried every wile imaginable to attract faculty and students of the first rank. And it involves the resurgence of the city itself, and of the Village in particular.

N.Y.U.'s professional schools of law, medicine and business have long been highly regarded, but today the university's unquestioned strengths include the Tisch School of the Arts, the Courant Institute of Mathematical Sciences, the Center for French Civilization and Culture, the Hagop Kevorkian Center for Near Eastern Studies, the Africana Studies Program, the Center for Neural Science and the Institute of Fine Arts, located off campus on East 78th Street.

"We have changed from a commuter school whose entrance requirements were in the medium range into a national university whose students come from all over the country and the world," said L. Jay Oliva, a professor of Russian history who became president of N.Y.U. in 1991. Setting the Goals A Billion Dollars In One Decade

N.Y.U.'s $1 billion drive was supposed to take 15 years. It took 10.

When undertaken back in 1984, it was a daring move. Not until 1992 did Stanford become the first university to complete a billion-dollar fund-raising drive. Harvard is now seeking $2 billion, and both Yale and Cornell are soon to complete five-year billion-dollar drives.

"A few years before, a major campaign at Yale had come close to failing," said Robert Ashton, vice president for development at the New School for Social Research in Greenwich Village. "And N.Y.U. didn't have a long history of alumni participation."

The university, like the city itself, had survived perilous financial trouble in the mid-70's. It was losing students to the expanding City University system, which still did not charge tuition. Things

had become so bad, N.Y.U. had to sell off a decrepit Bronx satellite campus to the state just to meet payroll in the spring of 1973. Four years later, the university again staved off financial trouble by selling, for $115 million, a macaroni company, Mueller, which it had acquired in the late 1940's.

Still, N.Y.U.'s future was precarious. Founded in 1831 as a private university for immigrants and the children of immigrants living in the New York metropolitan area, it was known as reliable but uninspired. The crumbling campus and paucity of dormitories doomed any effort to recruit students nationally.

By 1984, it became clear that the university had to do something big.

"We were mediocre," said President Oliva. "You can do well in this world if you're absolutely the best or if you're the best bargain, but not if you're somewhere in the middle. We were in a position where we had to grow or die."

Then chancellor, he and John Brademas, N.Y.U.'s president from 1980 to 1991, and Mr. Tisch, since 1978 chairman of N.Y.U.'s board of trustees, chose to go all out.

Mr. Tisch and his fellow trustees, many of whom had attended N.Y.U. as night-school students and could not afford an Ivy League education, were proud of their humble beginnings and pleased to show off their accomplishments. "By elevating N.Y.U.," Mr. Tisch, a 1942 graduate, said with a chuckle, "we made our degrees worth more."

But they also had a larger vision. Many of the trustees -- men like William R. Salomon, founder of Salomon Brothers Inc.; Walter V. Shipley, chairman of Chemical Bank, and Lewis T. Preston, former chairman of the J. P. Morgan Company -- were financiers with large stakes in the city. They understood the financial plight of New York well and were eager to do something about it.

"Although our main purpose was to help N.Y.U.," said Mr. Tisch, "We are citizens of New York. N.Y.U. is a real anchor for this city. If you include the medical center, it's one of the largest employers in town. We wanted to help both the university and the city." Raising the Money Major Gifts Up the Ante

The university's chief fund-raiser, Naomi B. Levine, took a pragmatic look at the membership of the board and saw dollars.

"I knew, for example, that Mr. Tisch and Leonard Stern, the owner of the Hartz Group, would soon make major gifts," Mrs. Levine said. "We also had on the board George Heyman of Lehman Brothers, who is one of the best fund-raisers in the city, and philanthropists like Lew Rudin of Rudin Management; Alan Greenberg, the chairman of

Bear, Stearns, and Morris Bergreen of the Skirball Foundation."

"You look at a group of trustees of that quality," Mrs. Levine said, "and you say to yourself no university has a better group and none has a more effective chairman than Larry Tisch."

The fund-raisers capitalized on the facts that Mr. Tisch almost never turned down a proposed meeting with a potential contributor and that as New Yorkers, they were never more than a cab ride away from the headquarters of most major foundations.

"The best way to raise money is not by having the best brochures, charts, fund-raising thermometers and so forth," said Mr. Oliva, "but to keep constantly on the road. Shoe leather!"

Despite such enthusiasm, the billion-dollar goal often seemed daunting. "We had to raise $2 million a week for 500 weeks," said President Oliva.

In 1988, the Tisch family made a $30 million donation. The same year, Leonard Stern contributed $30 million, and fund raising topped $90 million that year, for a total of $366 million. In 1989, contributions soared to $123 million, a record. The annual total slid down with the general economy over the next few years, but never fell below $100 million.

In 1991 came an odd bequest, the $25 million legacy of the actress Paulette Goddard. After all, she was a high school dropout from Great Neck, L.I., not an alumna, and lived most of her life in Hollywood and Switzerland. But behind the scenes were her dentist, Dr. Maurice Saklad, another N.Y.U. board member, and N.Y.U.'s president, Mr. Brademas, who speaks warmly of the "good chemistry" he had with Ms. Goddard.

Last year, N.Y.U. raised $116.5 million, and with that, the $1 billion mark was reached without even counting what may be the largest single gift ever given to an American university -- the late Sir Harold Acton's estate in Florence, La Pietra, valued at between $300 million and $500 million. N.Y.U. officials are not counting it yet because Sir Harold's will is still in probate.

Last week, the university celebrated reaching its goal with a black-tie affair at the Bobst Library on Washington Square. But of course, there were a few disappointments along the way.

"Our corporate contributions were not as strong as they should be," Mrs. Levine said. "The only overseas country that's been helpful has been Japan. We should have done much better in Germany and Italy," she said, given the Italian Studies Department and the Deutsches Haus on Washington Mews, a center for the study of German culture.

As Mr. Oliva sees it, there can be no letup. "When you raise this kind of money, you also raise the level of your expectations," he said. "That means continuing to raise $100 million a year. It's like what John Wooden said when he was coach of the U.C.L.A. basketball team. He said, 'A team doesn't stay the same. It either gets better or it gets worse.' I intend to get better." Spending It All Fat Wallet Buys Dorms and Deans

If fund raising was often a struggle, spending was a cinch. The largest share of the billion raised -- about $600 million -- was used to complete the expansion and renovation of the Washington Square campus.

Among the 22 buildings erected, bought or renovated were the $35 million Tisch School of the Arts, which opened in 1985, and the Department of Chemistry, which underwent a $15 million renovation between 1987 and 1989.

Equally important for an urban university like N.Y.U. were the 11 dormitories built or renovated. These included the $14 million Goddard Hall at 86 Washington Square East and the $49 million Carlyle Court complex on Union Square that was bought and renovated between 1987 and 1989.

Some students who came to live in these quarters were attracted by generous offers of financial aid, totaling $109 million. Others were lured by the new sense of urgency and growth that emanated from the university.

The infusion of money also made possible the energetic, decade-long recruitment of a stellar faculty to fill 88 new chairs. The hunt and capture was supervised by Duncan Rice, a Scotsman who was himself recruited in 1985 from Hamilton College, in upstate Clinton, by President Oliva. He is now vice chancellor.

N.Y.U. had the advantage of flexibility. Unlike many public colleges and universities where salaries are tied to rank, there was nothing to stop Mr. Rice and his colleagues from luring an associate professor, for instance, with a higher salary than that received by a full professor in the same department. Not all the new hires have been welcomed with open arms. Andrew Ross, who was drawn from Princeton in 1993 to head N.Y.U.'s American Studies Program, has faced criticism for his focus on such matters as gay and lesbian studies.

Mr. Rice, as dean of the faculty of arts and science, began to think systematically about recruitment, he said, soon after his arrival in 1985. That year, he learned that Anthony Movshon, a leading N.Y.U. specialist in neuroscience, was about to accept an offer from the Massachusetts Institute of Technology.

56

"It made me wonder about what we could do to persuade him to stay, and, if we succeeded, how we might use Movshon to attract other outstanding people in his field," Mr. Rice said. "I knew that neuroscience was one of the most rapidly expanding fields in the biomedical sciences -- people were talking about this being the Decade of the Brain -- and it seemed like an opportunity to create a center of strength."

Eventually, Mr. Rice persuaded Professor Movshon to stay by creating the Center for Neural Science, which gave him the unusual opportunity to hire 10 professors and develop what is now an internationally known center for the experimental and theoretical study of the human brain.

Other professors were lured by the promise of rejuvenating a troubled department. By the early 1990's, N.Y.U.'s department of political science had become a victim of internal strife, its staff pared as 6 of 27 faculty members quit. But the resignations meant that a new chairman would have the opportunity to reshape a department.

Russell Hardin, a leading expert on the role of morality in politics, was lured from the University of Chicago for the job. In the last year and a half, he has hired two faculty members from Stanford, one from Harvard, one from Princeton and one from the University of Chicago.

In another instance, a university asset proved to be the lure. John Freccero, a leading Dante scholar,

gave up a post at Stanford three years ago to move to N.Y.U. because of its Casa Italia. The landmark brownstone on West 12th Street between Fifth and Sixth Avenues is where the seven faculty members have their offices and conduct classes.

"Everybody acknowledges the importance of Italian culture in the Renaissance and so forth," said Professor Freccero, "but very few universities have a commitment to it to match N.Y.U.'s."

It also helped that Professor Freccero was baptized at Our Lady of Pompeii Roman Catholic Church on Carmine Street, and had warm memories of growing up in Greenwich Village. "New York City," he said, "was a big attraction for me."

As it is for so many others, says George E. Rupp, president of Columbia University. He says the city deserves some of the credit. "I am delighted with N.Y.U.'s progress," he said. "It reflects the resurgence of interest in New York City that we are all seeing, as more and more of the best students and faculty come here."

Said David Levitsky, 18, a film major at N.Y.U. from East Northport, L.I., "Many of my friends went to colleges with lawns and trees, but for me this is where it's happening."

A picture caption with the article misidentified the couple who were being greeted by L. Jay Oliva, the university's president, and Laurence A. Tisch, the chairman of CBS. They were Nan and Abraham Ellis, not Klara and Larry Silverstein

. *About the Archive*

RULE 13

Make Certain to Have a Program in Place for Corporation and Foundation Solicitations

In 2017 foundations gave $66.9 billion, which was 16% of total gifts made to charity in that year. In spite of the fact that this is a relatively small amount in relationship to the 70% that came from individuals, it is very important in the fundraising life of your organization. When a foundation gives you a grant it signifies that a group of very knowledgeable people in a peer review process approved your organization and the project you want funded. It is like a Good Housekeeping seal of approval. This inspires other donors to do the same.

Today there are approximately 82,516 foundations throughout the country. They must give away 5% of their assets each year. Some staff person in your organization must be responsible for foundations – studying their annual reports; what do they support; whom do they support; what do their guidelines say. Your organization must know the answers to these questions as they relate to many of the foundations that you believe would be willing to support you. You must look at their guidelines. You must try wherever possible to match their interests with yours. All of this information is accessible to the public through the Foundation Center. Every foundation must also issue an important annual report which lists the gifts that it made, the organizations it contributed to, and what guidelines it uses in making gifts.

At NYU we would also try to have the President meet the head of some of the major foundations, not to ask for money, but to get acquainted. If you are not in a position to meet with the president, you can meet with program directors and get acquainted with them. At such meetings you do not necessarily ask for money. You can simply get acquainted and provide information about the organization that you represent. That always helps. Keep in mind that foundations are looking for creative, innovative programs that can be easily evaluated. They do not fund endowment or organizational expenses. They fund projects and programs.

In planning your solicitation of a foundation, sometimes a phone call to the program officer will help. In some cases a letter of inquiry should be the first step. That letter should indicate the project you have in mind, why you think your organization is qualified to conduct it, the budget, and your desire to meet with someone at the foundation to discuss it further. If the response is positive, you then either meet with someone at the foundation or prepare a more detailed proposal. These proposals should not be fifty page dissertations. They should be brief and should explain succinctly what it is you want funded, why you think you are qualified to handle the project, why you believe it is unique, an explanation of the budget, how you plan to get other funds, and, again, how you plan to evaluate it. If you can get a meeting, of course, that is the best way to proceed. If not, you have to rely upon the proposals that you send in writing.

While the substance of your request is, of course, primary, good, clear, and succinct writing is also important. Nothing turns a foundation off more than a solicitation that misspells the salutation or contains sloppy grammar. "If they cannot get my name right, how can I expect them to administer my grant properly," is the usual response to a badly written proposal. Have your proposal proofread by a competent editor to prevent such an embarrassment.

Corporations do not give as much as foundations, but are another important source of income. In 2017 they gave $20.75 billion, which was 5% of the giving for that year. They give either cash, services, and, many times, equipment and products. More than one-third of corporate giving is in-kind. (For example, pharmaceutical companies are known for their contributions to medicine.) Some give directly from the corporation itself while others set up a foundation.

Corporations give for many reasons. Some want to be good citizens and others give because it is good for their business. Some give for both reasons. Some economists, like Milton Friedman, formerly of the University of Chicago, believe that corporations exist solely to make money for their stockholders. Others believe that corporations have a social responsibility to their community and to their country, as well. Most corporations in the United States follow this latter path and do assume, to some degree, their corporate social responsibility, but I have no doubt they also are motivated by the fact that it is good for their business.

There are about 1.2 million public corporations in the United States. Information about them is filed with the Securities and Exchange Commission and the Internet will provide you with that information. Each of them also put out annual reports, which again will give you a great deal of information about their interests and their charitable giving. Here, like with the foundations, it is important to keep your proposals short, succinct, and well written. It is best to go to those corporations that do business in your community. Most corporations like to make their charitable gift where they are located. If a bank has a branch in your area, it is more likely that branch will contribute to you than to some organization in another community. Keep this in mind when you decide on which companies to approach.

Do not concentrate your request for gifts on large corporations only. Recent reports indicate that smaller businesses also make contributions. Indeed, there are reports indicating there is a new emerging interest in philanthropy among small and mid-size firms. Do not neglect, therefore, these firms in your solicitations. These firms also provide the largest number of volunteers and people who volunteer give more money to charity than people who do not volunteer.

"An accumulating body of evidence suggests that the fastest-growing segment of philanthropy in the for-profit sector is small and midsize business. Until recently, this nascent trend has been hard to detect. The principal sources of data on corporate giving – the Council on Federal Aid to Education, the Conference Board, and the Council on Foundations – have been concentrated exclusively on companies with at least 500 employees and $100 million of revenue. We know much less about the charitable habits of firms with fewer than 500 employees, even though they account for 53% of all paid employment in America, than we do about the Fortune 500. But now research has revealed how critical the role of smaller firms has become to business giving. Three studies point to their centrality in the years ahead. Our ignorance is beginning to dissipate.

"One new inquiry was devoted to examining small and medium-sized business giving habits in the states of Indiana and Oregon. It found that firms with fewer than 500 employees and $10 million of revenue donate at least as much per employee and as a percent of net income as do larger firms. The importance of that funding is magnified when one considers that small businesses, already dominant in industries like wholesale trade, retail trade, and construction, are currently the fastest growing segment of commercial firms in America."[4]

Studies also show that what most influences small businesses in making a philanthropic gift are the values of the owner and, of course, the condition of his business. If business is poor, there will be no gifts in spite of the owner's values.

The current economy does not augur well for corporate profits, but one can only hope it is cyclical and will improve.

More recently, there has been an increase in sponsorship (the bulk of which is for sports) and cause-related marketing. The latter is defined as a company providing money to a nonprofit in direct proportion to the quantity of product purchased by consumers during that period. For example, if the Breast Cancer Research Foundation has an arrangement with Lauder cosmetics company, the Lauder company will give X amount of money to the foundation depending on the amount of Lauder products that are sold during that special campaign. The nonprofit gets the additional money and the company gets the publicity. Clearly, corporate giving improves the image that the company has within the community and that goodwill is indispensable in projecting the company's products. All surveys show that there is a strong relationship even during economic downturns between the amount of nonprofit activity the company is engaged in and the interest of consumers in their product.

---

[4] Clotfelter, Charles T. and Thomas Ehrlich, Eds. Philanthropy and the Nonprofit Sector in a Changing America. Indiana: Indiana University Press, 1999. (pg.107)

RULE 14
Understanding How and Whom to "Ask"

The "Ask" is probably the most important part of any fundraiser's responsibility. It requires careful preparation, thorough knowledge about what the "ask" entails, and as much information as possible about the prospective donor. Most fundraisers, including presidents, board members, and volunteers, are very uncomfortable with asking for money. Some of them are absolutely terrified. They would much prefer to write a letter than to have a meeting at which they actually have to ask for money. The best approach, I believe, is one that does not "ask for money." Instead, one asks for support for a particular project. Now, let me be personal for a moment. While it is difficult or impossible for me to ask for money for myself, it is not difficult to ask for something that I believe is of importance. Always keep this in mind when you are making an "ask" and keep in mind that a rejection is not a personal rejection, but rather a rejection concerning a project or a program. One cannot take these rejections personally. One has to view them within the context of what fundraising is all about.

To help you feel comfortable about the "ask" and to feel confident in yourself, it is important that you prepare carefully and that you have as much knowledge as possible about the prospective donor and the project you want funded. Some people suggest that you prepare a written script before the meeting and go over it several times, so that you feel comfortable with the approach you will use. This is often a valuable technique.

When exactly the "ask" should be made is hard to answer. Each ask is so different. One has to have a "feel" for when the situation is ready for asking for support. Usually it comes after a period of cultivation. Only the "asker" can ascertain when this should occur.

When a decision has been made to "ask," a quiet place should be chosen. The asker should speak with confidence. Never apologize for asking and let the donor speak. Once you make your request, stop talking. Let the prospective donor respond. How he or she responds will determine what your future strategy should be.

Whether the gift is made or not, be sure to thank the prospective donor. Follow up with a letter and/or a call to thank him for his time and, if possible, set another date to discuss the gift further or to answer questions raised that the asker could not respond to adequately.

Don't give up, even if the answer is "no." You may have learned something more about the prospect which will help you in further relationships.

May I suggest that every fundraiser buy the book by Laura Fredricks called "The Ask." It is the most comprehensive book on this subject that covers every aspect of "the ask." The most important point it makes, and I support this strongly, is to never "ask for money." Instead, ask for "support" for a project or program.

In the book, Laura Fredricks suggests:

- "understand thoroughly the program you want supported;

- judge the prospect's readiness for the ask;

- select the right person or team to do the ask;

- prepare carefully for the ask."

In the meeting with the donor be sure you let the prospective donor talk to you of his life and his interest in your organization, so that you have a feeling about this donor; that you understand his interests; and how those interests are part of your organization's objectives. In brief, listen. Do not talk. Your "ask" is more effective if you make the ask in relationship to the donor's interests.

This is important. People give to people and the right person asking is critical. Try to choose someone the prospective donor knows and, of course, respects.

It is almost impossible to really know when a donor is ready for an "ask." It is almost like trying to determine when it is ready to ask: "Will you marry me?" It is a feeling, an emotional sensitivity. Always keep in mind the quicker you ask, the less you will get. Take your time. Know the donor. Be sensitive to his or her interests. And remember if the donor turns you down, it is not personal. It is not a rejection of you. Keep your relationship going. As I said above: write to the donor; keep the donor informed on what is happening in your organization; send the donor memorandum, brochures and press releases so the donor keeps in touch with you. You never know when he or she may change their mind

RULE 15
Technology

Obviously, the use of technology in every form is critical in fundraising. It can provide you with much information as is available about a prospective donor. You cannot go out and visit with a prospective donor, or even write to then, without knowing about him or her. A computer search should be able to give you their biography, information about their career, information about their marriage and family, their finances, interests, and to what organizations they have contributed. As a civil libertarian, I hate that, but as a fundraiser, as I said above, it is critical.

In addition to giving you information about a potential donor, computers make it possible to:

- Keep records of every meeting you have with a donor, including where the meeting was held, when you met, what letters were sent, what replies were received, and any comments in writing that you or the donor made.

- Maintain documents describing any programs or projects you suggested to the donor and any responses he or she made.

- Record any "ask" that was made and the response.

- Document all interactions with a donor and descriptions of the next possible steps.

Technology is also used to advertise your organization and to ask for funds. This is a new addition to fundraising. Some of the videos put online are very moving and can help immeasurably in interesting people in your organization and in giving you visibility. Asking for money online is now a very common method of solicitation. I do not believe that it gets "major gifts" which require personal attention to the donor, but it is certainly helpful in getting smaller donations.

Technology is very much related to how your image is projected. How you appear on the web is critical. At NYU we consider our webpage as the public face of the University. We have hundreds of professors on the website describing themselves and their courses. We have pictures of our dormitories, our labs, our sports center, etc. You can and must do the same with your organization. This is especially important for younger people.

One last word: technology is changing every day. New instruments, new technology, and new ideas of how to use the technology are coming to the fore with increasing rapidity. As I said earlier, I am not one who "sells books," but whenever I find a book that adds an important contribution, I urge you to read it. Either buy it or borrow it from a nonprofit's library. The book is "Mobile For Good," by Heather Mansfield, an expert in social media.

I confess here that this is not an area in which I am an expert. I must depend on those who are. These areas are very important and as Heather Mansfield says, "Even if you can only invest 5 staff hours and a mobile and social media budget of $1,000 annually, your nonprofit must invest in mobile and social media."

To give you some idea of what this book covers I am quoting below the description of its contents from the inside cover of the book jacket:

"Mobile devices are fast becoming the #1 means of digital communication. If you want a sustainable future for your nonprofit, you need to have a strong presence on prospective donors' tablets and smartphones.

"Statistics prove that the most successful online fundraising campaigns are those designed for portable devices – from 2-inch smartphone screens to 17-inch laptops. In this groundbreaking book, social media pioneer Heather Mansfield offers everything you need to know to conceptualize, build, and maintain a mobile and social fundraising strategy to dramatically increase donations.

"In *Mobile for Good*, Mansfield takes you step by step through the entire process. Learn how to:

o Master your mobile fundraising strategy

o Create a strategic plan flexible enough to handle changes in technology

o Design a website and emails that work on both mobile devices and computers

o Choose the best mobile and online tools based on your budget and your donor demographics

o Build a system that tracks, evaluates, and reports campaign results

66

   o Maximize the potential of Facebook, Twitter, LinkedIn, and other sites

"Whether your goal is to raise more funds online, launch a new program, or increase your capacity to maintain current operations, creating and executing a mobile and social media strategy is a small investment that packs a big punch. Apply the lessons of *Mobile for Good*, and your organization can and will raise more funds than ever."[5]

Having read the book, I thoroughly agree.

Because the world of technology is moving so quickly, I find that as soon as I finish writing a section on technology a new book with new ideas and a new approach for using social networking and the web for charities is published. I find that there are new ideas for people now entering fundraising.

Because of my age, I am not literate in the latest ideas in the world of social networking and I find I must rely on the best books that come out that explore this world in detail. One of those books just reached my desk today. It is called *People to People Fundraising: Social Networking and Web 2.0 for Charities*, by Ted Hart, James M. Greenfield, and Sheeraz D. Haji. It describes the new tools to help nonprofit organizations increase their financial support. It teaches you how to tap into the many opportunities of social networking on the web with "practical, hands-on techniques and case studies." It is written by a team of internationally respected names in the field and it highlights new philanthropic examples from around the world "illustrating how individuals have leveraged the power of the Internet to move great numbers of others to support a charity or cause."

The book talks about the "changing nature of the community; the Internet to build relationships; expand the reach of an organization; why site benchmarking is a useful technique; leveraging social networking to further an organization's mission; people to people fundraising, marketing strategy, special events, relationships, and online marketing."

May I urge that you read this book and buy it if possible.

---

[5]Mansfield, Heather. *Mobile for Good*. McGraw-Hill Education, 2014.

RULE 16

Fundraisers Must be Knowledgeable About the Laws that Govern Nonprofits and Be Sensitive to Ethical Issues

At a time when the media are reporting almost daily stories of bad management, board negligence, excess salaries, fraudulent telemarketing and even criminal behavior in nonprofit organizations, it is imperative that fundraisers be knowledgeable about the laws that govern nonprofits and be especially sensitive to ethical issues involved in fundraising. Since donor trust in nonprofits, moreover, is less than 20% today, it is important that such knowledge be part of a fundraiser's qualifications.

More than any other group, fundraisers know that trust and donor confidence is critical to any fundraising effort. "If Americans cannot trust their charities," says Mark Everson, former Commissioner of Internal Revenue, at a hearing of the Senate Finance Committee, "they will stop giving and people in need will suffer." Furthermore, Senator Charles Grassley, former chairman of the Senate Finance Committee stated:

> "The charitable community should not stand silently by the sidelines when the newspapers are filled with flagrant waste and abuse at charity organizations. I am troubled that there is no criticism from the charitable community about the serious problems at American University and the Getty Foundation. Charitable leaders must be a strong voice in condemning inappropriate behavior in their sector."[6]

Such a strong voice can only come about if fundraisers are made sensitive to these issues. Most fundraisers are so busy raising money, meeting their goals

---

[6] Charles Grassley, "Remarks" (Committee on Finance 2005 Independent Sector Annual Conference, CEO Summit, October 25, 2005).

and finding prospects, that rarely do they sit down and consider the ethical issues in what they are doing or even to study the laws that govern their organizations. I urge fundraisers to take courses in these subjects. Such courses are now given at many universities and by many fundraising organizations. It is true that most fundraisers are honest, hardworking, committed and trustworthy human beings. But even such honest and decent human beings require additional education about their work if they are to continue to be effective. Any hint of subterfuge or unethical behavior in the fundraising profession surely kills donor generosity. Sensitivity and education can often prevent this. Time should be spent, therefore, at development meetings to talk about ethical and legal issues. This is as important in assuring the success of your campaign as the numbers you raise.

One foolish mistake, one act of unethical behavior, can ruin a campaign. The problems at the Red Cross, the Baptist Foundation of America, the Smithsonian Institution, United Way of America, Adelphi University, the Getty Foundation, and Sloan Kettering Hospital, to mention a few, demonstrate the problems an organization faces when unethical behavior is disclosed.

An examination of just a few of these cases indicate that they all point to the negligence of the board, boards that were uninvolved in any aspect of the administration, ignorant of the financial health of the organization, and dismissive of the responsibilities they have in supervising the CEO or executive director. They also show, in the Baptist case and the Nature Conservancy case, what happens when boards forget the importance of conflict of interest statements and take advantage of their role as leaders in a nonprofit organization to make a profit or gain an advantage form the organization's activities. It is very important as you read these cases to make certain that your organization has an appropriate Conflict of Interest statement.

- The resignation of William Aramony, of the United Way, in disgrace for the misuse of United Way funds, for hiring chauffeur driven cars, taking the Concorde on trips to Europe, visits to places where there was no United Way business – including 29 trips to Las Vegas, England, France, Norway, Turkey, Germany, Russia, and Italy – is a dramatic example of a board's failure to supervise its director and scrutinize his expenses. After a difficult trial, which was an embarrassment to United Way and to Mr. Aramony, he was sentenced to prison for seven years.

- The Adelphi University incident is also a case of special interest. The President, Dr. Peter Diamandopoulos, bought a luxury condominium with university funds for $1.2 million in New York City, plus furnishings and artwork worth $905,000. He also bought a condominium in Garden City at the cost of $400,000 and a personal collection of art appraised at over $700,000. All of this was paid for with university funds. He was paid, in addition, $523,636 in salary, plus benefits, deferred compensation, etc. On the request of faculty, hearings were held by the New York State Board of Regents. As a result of the hearings, the Adelphi University Board was asked to resign and the Trustees were condemned for lack of oversight and for giving him an outrageous salary package. Eventually, the Regents and Adelphi worked out an agreement where Adelphi received $3.5 million in insurance, plus $1.23 million from the former Trustees themselves. The Trustees also had to pay more than $400,000 in legal bills. Diamandopoulos was forced to refund more than $650,000 to Adelphi and paid more than $100,000 in rent on the Manhattan apartment, which he also agreed to vacate. He was forced to resign and a new president was installed.

- The Baptist Foundation of America is another case worth studying. This foundation went bankrupt, was shut down amid scandals, lies, and financial losses. It was involved in real estate deals for insiders, speculative land deals and squandered money on lavish offices, inflated salaries and fancy automobiles for staff. Directors borrowed money, violating the self-dealing rule and made profit from the various deals it made with the foundation. The foundation rarely if ever revealed its financial status. The Phoenix Times stated: "State officials have determined that the Baptist Foundation of America is thought to have perpetrated the largest scam in U.S. history." (October 21, 1999)

- The Nature Conservancy is another example of where conflict of interest was not sufficiently obeyed. The Nature Conservancy is the largest environmental charity in the United States with assets of more than $3 billion. It is a highly respected nonprofit organization with the mission of "preserving plants, animals and natural communities that represent the diversity of life on earth by protecting the land and water they need to survive." The Nature Conservancy buys or receives land and often holds it in perpetuity to make certain it will be forever wild. Its reputation has always been superb and above reproach. Imagine the shock when the Washington Post reported a series of unusual arrangements the Nature Conservancy made with board members that inured to the profit of the board member.

In short, the Nature Conservancy would buy some land that it wanted to keep undeveloped and put an easement on the land. This would reduce its value, which would for example make a $1 million dollar piece of property worth only $700,000. The Nature Conservancy would then sell the land to a donor for $700,000. The donor would then contribute $300,000 to the charity and take a charitable deduction for the $300,000. Sometimes the appraisal of the property was adjusted to make the tax deduction larger. Evidence showed this was an insider deal available only to those close to the chairman. Nothing illegal, Doug White states in his book *Charity on Trial*, but clearly an unethical tone. There was also evidence of loans to top ranking officials in the Nature Conservancy, including a loan of $1.5 million to the executive director to buy a house when he moved from California to Washington.

Doug White's comments on this case in his book *Charity on Trial* are worth repeating in full:

"Perception is always an important concern. There is an old adage about whether a decision should be made, or at least guided by, the concern about how it will look in tomorrow morning's newspaper. This is particularly true when the decision involves gray areas. A gray area would not involve a person receiving deduction for a gift, but whether that gift opportunity, in the context of who might be most interested in it, is available and made known to only a few people, a few friends.

"The Nature Conservancy forgot the adage, but it did something remarkable. Less than a month after the *Post* series was published, and before the Senate Finance Committee got into the act, the board at the Nature Conservancy met to discuss the newspaper's allegations.

"The board brought in outside help – people intimately knowledgeable about the way charities ought to run – and, after an independent report was issued – voted to make changes in the way the charity operated.

"The board made a new rule that barred board members, trustees, employees, and their immediate family members from taking part in the conservation buyer program.

"The board terminated its practice of providing loans to its employees.

"The board announced that it would use independent advisors to assist in its 'aspiration of making the Conservancy a recognized leader in governance and oversight.'

"Although it was wounded by the *Post* articles, the Nature Conservancy took them seriously. The board said, 'We are committed to changing any of our practices that do not live up to our mission and values.' There would be no more winking and nodding.

"The Nature Conservancy did not run and hide. Its board acted with speed, efficiency, and sensitivity to public opinion."[7]

- The tragedy of September 11, 2001 touched every part of American life and, of course, it involved hundreds of charities, some new and some old, with the Red Cross at the center. In less than four months the Liberty Defense Fund, created by the Red Cross to collect 9/11 contributions, raised more than $667 million. $2.7 billion was raised all told by charities for 9/11. The Red Cross itself raised $988 million. Of this money, $250 million was <u>not</u> allocated to 9/11 victims, but rather to other causes. Needless to say, many donors were outraged when they discovered this. They believed that the Liberty Defense Fund was created only to help 9/11 victims. They were dismayed that their money, donated for 9/11 was used for other purposes – even if the other purposes were important.

  As a result of this conflict, Congressional hearings were held. The Red Cross defended itself, saying that the mission statement of the LDF stated clearly that the money would be used for this tragedy and the emerging needs from this event. Congress did not buy this, as that phrase was in tiny letters on mission statements that had been distributed.

  The director of the Red Cross was forced to resign; Congress insisted on restructuring the Red Cross; the board, of course, was restructured, too; a new director was brought in; and the Red Cross now asks its donors specifically how they want their money spent. It is still too early to know if the trust the public had in the Red Cross, which was lost immediately after the 9/11 fiasco, has returned.[8]

And, as said repeatedly in this book: when trust is lost, your organization is dead. The cases of mismanagement and fraud that have come to the surface

---

[7]White, Doug. *Charity on Trial: What You Need to Know Before You Give.* New Jersey: Barricade Books, 2007. (page 154)

[8] Ibid. (page 163-178)

reveal that self-regulation of nonprofits, which the nonprofit world lobbies for, does not seem to have eliminated or curbed some appalling procedures. It might be time for donors, therefore, to demand more government regulations to strengthen charitable governance and to help ensure continued confidence and support for nonprofits.

I REPEAT: OF ALL THE RULES IN THIS BOOK, I CONSIDER THIS RULE, I.E., A CONCERN WITH ETHICAL ISSUES, BOARD GOVERNANCE AND KNOWLEDGE OF THE LAW, THE MOST IMPORTANT. IF YOU OR YOUR ORGANIZATION ARE EVER VIEWED AS UNETHICAL, SLEAZY, NOT TRUSTWORTHY, ALL THE RULES SET FORTH IN THIS BOOK ARE USELESS. INTEGRITY AND TRUST ARE THE HEART AND SOUL OF FUNDRAISING. EVERYTHING ELSE IS COMMENTARY.

Addenda

1. NYU: Planning Your Gift
2. Prospect Research Sources
3. Contemporary Problems in Philanthropy, by Naomi Levine

PLANNING *your* GIFT

Table of Contents

NEW YORK UNIVERSITY invites you to make a gift that will be a wise investment for you and your family, as well as for future generations of NYU students.

IN THIS BROCHURE, you will learn about creative gift planning arrangements that maximize financial advantages both for you and New York University. Your charitable gift can help you:

- Generate a high and secure income for life

- Pass more of your wealth to your family and loved ones

- Realize a substantial current year income tax charitable deduction

- Earn higher income while avoiding capital gains taxes

- Reduce or eliminate your estate tax burden

NYU GIFT PLANS are extremely flexible and can be tailored to fit your unique circumstances and needs. Your gift to NYU can become an integral part of your overall asset planning.

In this brochure, we will reveal unexpected possibilities and opportunities to combine your philanthropy with your financial and tax planning, so you can design your gift to maximize the advantages for you, your family, and for NYU.

We will be delighted to talk with you and your adviser, to help you explore which of these gift arrangements may best suit your needs.

3

Legacies through Your Will or Living Trust

Making a Difference through Your Bequest

By naming New York University in your will or living trust, you can realize substantial tax savings while continuing your support for the future of the University.

ESTATE GIVING has long been the most popular means of improving the lives of future generations of NYU students and teachers. Schoolteachers, dancers, accountants, engineers, lawyers, nurses, social workers, physicians, and business owners—the many faces of our alumni, with a diverse range of financial circumstances—have found it simple and appropriate to name NYU in their wills.

You can bequeath a specific dollar amount or a portion of what remains after your obligations to others are fulfilled. You can designate your bequest to support the University as a whole, or for a specific college or school. Through your bequest, you can establish and endow a permanent named fund for scholarships, program support, professorships, or the like.

4

You can include the University in your will or living trust by using the following language: "I give, devise and bequeath [assets/percent share of the residue of my estate] to New York University, a New York education corporation with its principal office at 70 Washington Square South, New York, New York 10012."

Please call us for additional language to ensure that the University will fulfill your wishes as you intend, or to discuss language that will establish a permanent named endowed fund for a particular purpose.

" Continue your support for the future of the University. "

5

Legacies through Your IRA, 401(k), or 403(b)

Tax-Wise Handling of Your Retirement Plan

Improve your estate's overall tax consequences and increase the amount of assets passing to your heirs by naming NYU as survivor beneficiary of your retirement plan, whether it is an IRA, 401(k), or 403(b).

YOUR RETIREMENT PLAN WORKS well for saving for retirement, but if you leave your retirement plan assets to your family and loved ones, those assets will be taxed much more heavily than other estate assets because those assets will be subject to income tax as well as any applicable estate tax.

Careful treatment of your retirement plan assets will avoid unnecessary tax costs. By naming NYU as survivor beneficiary of your retirement assets, your charitable gift will be exempt from both income and estate tax, effectively permitting you to make your gift at very low actual cost to your heirs. If you intend to leave a legacy to NYU through your will, prudent planning may call for you to make your gift primarily from your retirement account instead.

6

Here's how wise planning can benefit your heirs: George, a widower, is preparing his estate. His daughter is named as survivor beneficiary of his IRA, which contains $400,000. He also intends to leave NYU a generous gift of $400,000 through his will. George's legacy to NYU would result in no estate or income taxes. And although the IRA will pass to his daughter without estate tax, that gift will be subject to federal and state income tax when his daughter receives it, reducing the amount she receives from the IRA—potentially by as much as half its value.

However, if George rearranges his plans so that he bequeaths $400,000 to his daughter through his will, rather than through his IRA, and if he also designates NYU as survivor beneficiary of his IRA, then George's gifts to both NYU and his daughter will be free of all estate and income taxes. This tax-wise arrangement saves substantial taxes, to the overall advantage of George's daughter, and demonstrates the critical importance of thinking about the survivorship designation of your retirement plans in light of your overall estate planning.

7

Life-Income Gifts

Make a Gift that Pays You a High and Secure Income for Life

With a charitable life-income gift—such as the NYU Charitable Gift Annuity or a Charitable Remainder Trust—NYU will pay you a high and secure income for life, after which the University will use the remaining gift assets for the purpose you specify.

AN NYU LIFE–INCOME GIFT is particularly effective if you want to support the University and you also need to increase the income you currently receive from your assets.

There are also substantial tax advantages with a life-income gift. A large portion of your NYU income may be tax-free, and you obtain a significant income tax charitable deduction when you make your gift. If you make your contribution using appreciated stock, you avoid up-front capital gains tax, so that the full current value of your stock gift will be available to pay you a higher income.

NYU life-income gifts provide the flexibility that permits you to tailor an arrangement that best fits your financial needs. You can structure your gift to pay income to you or to loved ones. Income payments can begin immediately or can be deferred to a future date, such as your planned retirement.

8

Increase your income: Eileen, an alumna 82 years of age, wants to support NYU but she also wants to increase her retirement income. She contributes $100,000, and the University will pay her a secure income at a rate of 7.2% for the rest of her life. This amounts to an annual income of $7,200, of which $6,000 will be tax-free. When she makes her gift, she also obtains an income tax charitable deduction of over $50,000.

Unlock your appreciated stock for a higher income: Paul and Frieda, ages 77 and 74, want to increase the income from their stock holdings. They own stock worth $250,000, with a cost basis of $100,000. If they sell the stock outright and reinvest the proceeds, they would lose a substantial portion of their investment to capital gains taxes. However, when they transfer the stock to an NYU life-income gift, they avoid capital gains tax and the entire value of their gift asset will work to earn income for them. They select an income rate of 7%, increasing their income from $5,000 to $17,500. They also obtain an income tax charitable deduction of over $100,000, and ensure that future generations of students will benefit from their scholarship fund.

9

Increase your future retirement income: Lois, age 50, wants to save more for retirement, but she already contributed the maximum amount for the year to her employer's qualified retirement plan. She donates $10,000 to an NYU charitable gift annuity, directing that NYU begin to pay her income when she turns 70. NYU will pay Lois an annual income of $970, beginning in twenty years, for a rate of return of 9.7%. In addition, Lois obtains an income tax charitable deduction of about $2,600 in the year she makes the gift. With this gift, Lois increases her future retirement income. There is no limit on the amount Lois can contribute to this plan each year, and she can designate when the income payments will commence.

Leave a legacy of secure and high income to your spouse or heirs: Robert wants to leave a legacy to NYU to establish a scholarship fund, but he also wants to provide a source of income for his sister Margaret. He provides in his will for assets to pass to an NYU life-income gift that will pay a high and secure income to Margaret during her lifetime. This gift arrangement generates a substantial estate tax deduction, providing Margaret with even more income than if she received an outright taxable gift from Robert's estate. At Margaret's death, the remaining gift assets will be used by NYU to establish a named scholarship fund.

Note: Income and deduction figures are based on current tables and IRS rates and are subject to change.

> "NYU life-income gifts provide the flexibility that permits you to tailor an arrangement that best fits your financial needs."

11

Charitable Lead Trusts

Set Aside More Wealth for Your Heirs—And Provide an Income Stream to NYU

Individuals of substantial net worth can make a gift to New York University that will also ultimately leave more wealth to their family and heirs, with little or no tax.

THIS ARRANGEMENT, the Charitable Lead Trust, is designed to pay income to the University over a number of years. At the end of that time the remaining trust asset, including appreciation, passes to children or other designated heirs. Because the lead trust generates substantial tax savings, heirs can receive a greater inheritance than if the assets were left to them directly and fully subject to tax.

> " Heirs can receive a greater inheritance than if the assets were left to them directly. "

12

ANOTHER TYPE OF CHARITABLE LEAD TRUST can be designed
that returns the remaining trust assets to the donor after a specified
number of years. The donor sets an asset aside and provides that
its income passes to NYU for the trust's duration, after which the
assets pass back to the donor. In effect, this type of lead trust can
be thought of as a loan of the trust asset to NYU. This charitable
lead trust generates a substantial up-front income tax charitable
deduction for the donor in the year the trust is established. The
deduction is based upon the income that the trust will pay to
the University over the trust's term. This lead trust can be a
particularly powerful tool for donors who seek an immediate large
tax deduction to offset an unusually high taxable income in the
current year.

13

Gifts of Real Estate

Increase Your Tax Savings or Realize Income

You can contribute your home, vacation home, or commercial property to NYU. And you can make your gift in any of a number of ways to fit your needs and circumstances. You can contribute your entire property or a portion of it. You can make an outright gift of your property, or you can contribute it to an NYU life-income arrangement—avoiding capital gains tax and yielding an income tax charitable deduction, while eliminating management responsibilities and generating a high and secure source of income.

You can even contribute your personal residence but continue to reside there for the rest of your life. This type of gift—a future interest in your home—lets you continue to enjoy your home without diminishing your standard of living, while obtaining a substantial current income tax charitable deduction.

Give your home, but continue to live in it: Arnie and Annette, ages 73 and 68, own a home valued at $720,000. They make a gift of the home to NYU, while retaining the right to live there for the rest of their lives. While sustaining no change in their accustomed life-style, they increase their current cash flow because the charitable gift of NYU's future interest generates an immediate income tax charitable deduction of about $450,000.

Note: Deduction figures are based on current IRS tables and are subject to change.

14

Life Insurance Gifts

Leveraging Low Premiums into a Major Gift

WHEN PROPERLY ARRANGED, life insurance offers an attractive way to convert relatively low premium payments into a major gift to the University. If you no longer need all the life insurance that you own, you may want to name the University as a beneficiary. Any benefit the University receives from your insurance will be excluded from your taxable estate.

By taking the additional step of naming the University irrevocable beneficiary and owner of your life insurance policy, you can obtain an income tax charitable deduction equivalent to either the policy's cash surrender value or replacement value. If additional premium payments are due, you can deduct those premiums as charitable contributions each year.

15

NEW YORK UNIVERSITY invites you to join the Society of the
Torch, a special group of alumni, faculty, and friends who recognize
the importance of planning their philanthropy by providing for the
University and its schools and colleges through their wills or other gift
planning arrangements such as those described in this brochure.

The Society finds its inspiration in a ceremony conducted during
the University's commencement exercises, when a senior faculty
member passes the University torch to the youngest undergraduate
degree candidate. Just as the passing of the torch symbolizes the
continuity of learning, so membership in the Society honors
donors who share the foresight and commitment that enables the
University to fulfill its fundamental mission—passing the light of
knowledge to future generations.

Members of the Society receive complimentary invitations to
special University convocations, lectures, seminars, and other
events; information about current creative estate and tax planning
techniques; and frequent subscriptions to selected University
publications such as the *NYU Alumni Magazine*.

If you have previously provided for the University in your will
or trust, we would like to know of your generosity. Please take a
moment to call or write to us, and we will enroll you as a member
of the Society of the Torch.

16

Request
Further
Information

The University's Office of Gift Planning welcomes the opportunity to work with you and your advisers in planning your gift.

WE CAN PROVIDE sample language for your review in drafting your legacy and in establishing the terms of the restricted use of your gift so that it effectively reflects your own desires and objectives for the University's students and faculty. And we can offer calculations and illustrations of the tax and income benefits you may enjoy from your gift.

Your planned gift or bequest helps ensure that the New York University torch will continue to shine brightly for generations to come.

Please contact the Office of Gift Planning to discuss membership in the Society or to request information about how your gift can best fit your financial circumstances.

New York University
Office of Gift Planning
25 West Fourth Street, 4th Floor
New York, NY 10012-1119

Phone: 212-998-6960
Email: gift.planning@nyu.edu
Web: nyu.plannedgiving.org

17

 **NEW YORK UNIVERSITY**

New York University
Office of Gift Planning
25 West Fourth Street, 4th Floor
New York, NY 10012-1119

Phone: 212-998-6960
Email: gift.planning@nyu.edu
Web: nyu.plannedgiving.org

Prospect Research Sources

ONLINE:

Lexis-Nexis

1. People
2. Company
3. News
4. Assets

BOOKS/CD-ROMS/OTHER

1. FC Search
2. Leadership Directories
3. Social Registry
4. Directory of Directors
5. Rich Books (Who's Wealthy in America, etc.)
6. Forbes 400 and other lists
7. Annual Report

Information About Companies and Executives:

Hoovers.com

Hoovers provides directory information on thousands of companies, public and private. Information includes company descriptions, a list of top executives, address, phone, sales, stock data and links to other Web-based resources related to your search. Please note that certain parts of the site require a password.

Edgar.com

EDGAR is one of the most useful sites for business research on the Web. It provides documents electronically filed with the SEC (Securities & Exchange Commission). Use those documents to find salaries, stockholdings, and business histories on top executives and directors.

Information About Foundations:

Fdncenter.org

The Foundation Center has long been a leader in providing resources to the philanthropic community. Their site includes links to more than 600 foundation/corporate grant makers.

They also have a searchable directory called the "Foundation Finder."

Guidestar.org & Grantsmart.org

These sites provide basic information on 600,000 charities and nonprofits. Detailed information regarding assets, giving, sample grants, and officers can be found in the Form 990.

Information About Professionals:

Martindale-Hubbell.com

Their "Lawyer Locator" is a good resource for information on law firms and biographical information on attorneys.

Ama-Assn.org

"Doctor Finder" is complied and published by the American Medical Association as a reference source of demographic and professional information on individual physicians in the United States.

FECinfo.com

Use this site to find out contributions to Federal election candidates. There are several useful indexes including donor name, candidate name, and donor code.

Phone and Mail Directories:

Att.com

AT&T's phone directory has search tools for people, businesses, reverse lookup (by phone, not address) and toll free numbers.

USPS.com

The United States Postal Service's site provides company address information, zip codes for specific addresses, postal rates and other USPS information.

New York University
School of Continuing and Professional Studies

Contemporary Problems in Philanthropy

"The Advocate"*
and Other Essays
By Naomi Levine

Chair and Academic Director
of the George H. Heyman, Jr.
Center for Philanthropy
and Fundraising

NYU SCPS
SCHOOL OF CONTINUING & PROFESSIONAL STUDIES
At the center of the center of it all.

George H. Heyman, Jr.
Center for Philanthropy
and Fundraising

* Reprinted with permission from

Contribute
New York
:the people and ideas of giving

Contents

Essays on Contemporary Problems in Philanthropy Written by Naomi Levine

Published by *Contribute New York*

Published and Distributed by the George H. Heyman, Jr. Center for Philanthropy and Fundraising

Introduction

There are today 1.8 million nonprofit organizations in the United States. In 2007, they raised slightly more than $300 billion, an incredible amount. This "third sector" of American society plays an incredibly important role in the way our society functions. Hospitals, universities, museums libraries, performing and visual arts groups, social services for the poor, the aged, the ill, etc., all depend on this sector for their survival.

Yet this very important sector in which so much money is involved and in which so much in our society depends is only moderately regulated. In business and in government, on the other hand, there are scores of laws and regulations that provide oversight and supervision. And any attempt to increase the oversight of nonprofits is met with strong opposition from the nonprofits who insist "self regulation" not government regulation, is sufficient to assure that the sector is managed properly.

The articles in this monograph take issue with this, and support more regulation, more donor protection, more disclosure, and more accountability. In taking this position, the articles raise some controversial issues not merely on regulation vs. self-regulation, but on related issues such as the role of so-called "new" donors, on conflict of interest, on donors' rights, and global philanthropy.

These issues are controversial and deserve to be discussed more openly in the philanthropic world. Hopefully, articles such as these will encourage such discussion and debate. The opinions in all of the articles are mine and represent neither New York University nor *Contribute New York* magazine.

Naomi Levine

advocate
CONTINUED

"Just as the corporate world stood largely silent in the Enron debacle, leaders of the nonprofit world have done little to further nonprofit reform."

But the recent history of corporate America demonstrates that self-regulation has not worked. There is little reason to believe it will work any better in the nonprofit sector.

Many of the provisions of Sarbanes-Oxley can be applied to nonprofits at minimal additional cost to them. For example:

1 Board membership should require financial literacy training.

2 Nonprofits with budgets of more than $500,000 should assess the benefits and costs of annual audits.

3 All nonprofits that conduct outside audits should have an Audit Committee separate from the Financial Committee. The Audit Committee should be directly responsible for hiring, setting compensation and overseeing the activities of the auditors, and for reporting on the audit to the full board.

4 All nonprofits should ensure that no member of the staff, including the chief executive officer, should serve on the Audit Committee, although it is reasonable to have the key financial officer provide staff support to the Audit Committee.

5 Auditors should be rotated every five years and no auditing firms should provide non-auditing services, such as bookkeeping, financial information systems, appraisal, management, human resources, investment or legal services.

6 The chief executive officer and the chief financial officer should certify the organization's financial report, with the board having ultimate financial responsibility. Audited financial statements must be available to the board.

7 Every nonprofit organization should have a Conflict of Interest statement and every board member should sign it.

8 No board member should ever receive loans from the nonprofit organization.

9 The IRS should be prepared to receive Forms 990 and 990-PF filed electronically.

Many of these suggestions for the nonprofits were recently incorporated into a report by the Panel on the Nonprofit Sector created on the recommendation of the Senate Finance Committee. The panel—with input from many of the most important leaders in the world of philanthropy— issued its report in June 2005, but there has been little public debate about the panel's findings in the nonprofit community.

Perhaps it's time to hear from the donors.

Just as the corporate world stood largely silent in the Enron debacle, leaders of the nonprofit world have done little to further nonprofit reform. In October 2005, Senator Grassley said:

"The charitable community should stop standing silently on the sidelines when the newspapers are

"Every nonprofit should have a Conflict of Interest statement and every board member should sign it."

filled with stories of flagrant waste and abuse at a charity. I'm troubled that there was little to no criticism from the charitable community about the serious problems at American University and the Getty Foundation. Charitable leaders must be strong-voiced in condemning inappropriate behavior in their sector."

So I end this column as I began: If the leadership of the nonprofit community fails to speak out on necessary reform in board governance and transparency, it is time—in fact, past time—to hear from the donors. ◢

Naomi Levine is chair and executive director of New York University's George H. Heyman Jr. Center for Philanthropy and Fundraising and a regular columnist for this magazine. Her next column will appear in the May/June issue. Please send comments about this column to editors@contributemedia.com.

19%
The percentage of 1,820 Americans surveyed who said charities were doing a very good job running their programs and services.
Source: NYU's Robert F. Wagner Graduate School of Public Service

advocate
NAOMI LEVINE

Defending the Old Guard

New-age philanthropists who say nonprofits should be run more like businesses are missing the point

Naomi Levine

The distinction that is currently being made in the media between "old" and "new" philanthropists baffles me. These articles attribute to the "new" philanthropists a desire to be a genuine part of the projects they support, to know how their money is being spent and to support innovative ideas—not simply the status quo.

But does anyone believe that the "old guard" philanthropists are radically different from their new-age counterparts? Indeed, isn't the old guard just as interested in making the world a better place as these so-called new philanthropists? Without the "old generation" of philanthropists—from the Carnegies and Rockefellers to the present day—we would have few of

the major museums, hospitals, universities and other institutions that make our lives here in New York and around the country and the world so much better. Indeed, there are almost 2 million nonprofit institutions in the United States today and most of them were established by the "older generation." It is the philanthropy of the "older generation" that continues to provide food for the hungry, homes for the homeless and the myriad safety net services essential for the poor in this nation and around the world.

And isn't the old guard just as interested in knowing how the dollars are being spent as is the new-age philanthropist? In my 25 years at New York University, raising more than $2.5 billion for the university, I never received a gift without the donor wanting to be involved and expecting regular reports on the uses of that money. Most major donors become members of the advisory committees established to implement their projects, and many become members of the Board of Trustees of NYU so they can be involved not only in their individual projects, but in the direction of the university as a whole.

And donors have always sought to give —with strings attached. I have never been involved in a major gift without protracted discussions with the donor to assure that the monies contributed meet both the donor's best hopes and the institution's needs. Indeed, I consider it part of my professional responsibility as a fundraiser to discuss with donors the nature and uses of their gifts. I have yet to meet a prospective donor who hands me a blank check and says "goodbye."

To say, moreover, as some articles report, that the new philanthropists want to make philanthropy more "businesslike" (so that the nonprofits can be as efficient as corporations in America's private business sector) amazes me. Are they talking about General Motors, the airlines, the Ford Motor Company, the steel industry, private agricultural farms that need subsidies from the government to make a profit? Are they talking about Enron, WorldCom, Tyco? Are they talking about the corruption, greed and absolutely disgraceful salaries that some of the CEOs in private industry are making? Are they suggesting that the nonprofit sector look to the profit sector for examples of efficiency and ethical behavior? I doubt it.

I find it particularly disturbing to read such statements as those in a recent article in *The Economist* that asserted: "The new philanthropists rightly insist on making their money go further, because in the past, a lot of donors' cash has been wasted." It is true that some of the projects that donors have funded have not always reached the goals they set. But this does not necessarily mean that their cash has been wasted. Innovation and experimentation in the search for more effective ways of dealing with the difficult social, environmental and medical problems that face us are a basic function of philanthropy. Because philanthropists are not bound by pressures from voters or shareholders, they can try new ways of doing things. Obviously, some of these approaches will not succeed. But to say this is wasting money misses the point on why philanthropy, and the experiments it funds, is so important.

> It is time for "old guard" and "new" philanthropists to work together for reform so that what has plagued corporate America does not infect nonprofits.

Now, I do not mean to infer that foundations and other forms of philanthropy should not be supervised more effectively by the government. In line with this, Senate Finance Committee Chairman Charles Grassley has stated repeatedly that "in Congress, we need to do more oversight to make sure the checks and balances work and supervise the tax credits we're giving. We give tax deductions for charitable giving, so there's a public policy interest in how the money gets used." He also has pointed out that "those who turn a blind eye to the problems in the charitable sector or seek only a fig leaf of reform, potentially cause real long-term damage to nonprofits." What is needed, the senator warns, is "real reform to help ensure continued public confidence and support for nonprofits."

I think Senator Grassley is correct in wanting real reform in the governance of nonprofits. He is also correct, in my view, to suggest that many of the provisions of Sarbanes-Oxley be applied to the nonprofit world. This would require that boards be more active in the supervision and operation of the institutions; that they know what their executives are paid; that they demand greater disclosure and accountability and that whistle-blowers be protected—to name a few of Senator Grassley's suggestions.

Rather than jostle for the last word, it is time for "old guard" philanthropists and so-called "new-age" philanthropists to join together to work for these and other reforms to ensure that the corruption and mismanagement that has plagued corporate America in this post-Enron era does not infect nonprofits. All philanthropists—whether we call them old or new—have a critical role to play in this effort and a critical stake in the outcome.

Defending Nonprofits

There is one aspect of the "new" philanthropists' approach to philanthropy, however, that deserves special attention. In much of what they say and in many articles written about them, there is the assertion that the source of new ideas and creativity resides only outside major communal institutions. This is an assumption I believe is not true. No one has a monopoly on creativity. New ideas and new approaches sprout in many places and in the heads of many individuals, whether such individuals are working in established organizations or creating new ones. Indeed, many of the most creative ideas have sprouted within existing organizations—organizations which many of the "new" philanthropists would view as stodgy and frozen in the status quo. What the community needs today is for these "new" philanthropists not to deride the established communal organizations, but to work where it is appropriate in partnership with them—exchanging ideas, strategizing over programs and problems, exploring and evaluating what is being done and what should be done. In this way, each can learn from the other. Where such partnerships have existed, the whole community benefits. ◢

Naomi Levine is chair and executive director of NYU's George H. Heyman Jr. Center for Philanthropy and Fundraising and a regular columnist for *Contribute*. Her next column will appear in the July/August issue.

How often do you donate any money to nonprofit charitable causes?

18-29 years old:

41.2%   27.5%
20.8%
10.5%

30-49 years old:

34.6%   49.9%
12.3%   2.9%

50-64 years old:

37.3%   50.2%
10.1%   2.5%

65-plus years old:

36.8%   50.2%
8.3%   4.4%

KEY:

■ FREQUENTLY
■ OCCASIONALLY
■ RARELY
■ NEVER

Source: Zogby International, New York

advocate
NAOMI B. LEVINE

Hold the Phone

Telemarketers pocket a whole lot more than they give to charity—and it's legal. Here's why.

"I believe that a simple request for money lies far from the core protections of the First Amendment as heretofore interpreted."

— The late U.S. Supreme Court Justice William H. Rehnquist

Naomi B. Levine

Did you know that the bulk of the money you donate to a charity may go to the telemarketing company that solicits you—and not to the charity you think you are supporting?

Did you know that efforts by lawmakers to limit the amount of money that fundraisers or telemarketing companies can pocket for themselves have been consistently declared unconstitutional by the U.S. Supreme Court? Strange as it may seem, the Court seems to be more interested in protecting the fundraiser than in protecting the donor.

Let me explain. Under current law, and as a result of a series of Supreme Court cases beginning in 1980, the following rules are on the books:

: Professional fundraisers or telemarketing com-

panies can keep as much as 90 percent or more of the money they collect for their own expenses—giving very little to the charity involved.

: A fundraiser can't be limited in the amount of money he or she can charge.

: A state cannot require a fundraiser to be licensed.

: A state cannot require that a fundraiser disclose how much of the money collected during the previous year was used for program and administrative expenses.

: A state cannot limit the amount an organization can spend on fundraising. Organizations also can't be required to disclose this information to a donor— that is, if the donor doesn't ask.

How can this be? All of these protections for the fundraiser, telemarketer, and charity are the result of decisions by the Supreme Court that classify the solicitation of funds as "speech" protected by the First and Fourteenth Amendments. This principle was set forth by the Court in four cases, about which every donor, fundraiser, and charity should know. They are:

1 Village of Schaumburg v. Citizens for a Better Environment (444 U.S. 620; 1980) Schaumburg, Ill., passed an ordinance in 1974 prohibiting door-to-door and on-the-street solicitations of charitable contributions unless the charity uses at least 75 percent of its receipts for "charitable purpose." *The Supreme Court held that such an ordinance was unconstitutional, because such solicitations are "protected speech" within the purview of the First Amendment.*

2 Secretary of State of Maryland v. J.H. Munson Co. (467 U.S. 947; 1984) Maryland passed a law prohibiting a charity from paying, as expenses, more than 25 percent of the amount raised. *The Supreme Court declared this unconstitutional under the First and Fourteenth Amendments.*

3 **Riley v. National Federation of the Blind of North Carolina, Inc.** (487 U.S. 781; 1988) A North Carolina law defined a reasonable fee for a professional fundraiser. It said that a fee of up to 20 percent of receipts collected was reasonable. A fee of more than 35 percent was presumed unreasonable, but the fundraiser might rebut the presumption by showing that the situation involved dissemination of information or that this amount was necessary for the charity to raise the money it needed. The North Carolina statute also required that fundraisers be licensed and that they must disclose to potential donors the average percentage of gross receipts turned over to the charity within the previous 12 months. *All of these provisions to protect the donor were declared unconstitutional under the free speech protection.*

4 **Madigan v. Telemarketing Associates, Inc.** (538 U.S. 600: 2003) The telemarketing company kept slightly more than $6 million of $7 million raised for a Vietnam veterans group. The Court said this was not fraud. It said the company could be charged with fraud only if the solicitor made a misleading statement. However, if he simply asked for the money and made no comment about how much was going to the charity, he could not be charged with fraud. But in this case, the fundraiser said 90 percent or more went to the veterans in response to a question, and therefore could be charged with fraud.

The late U.S. Supreme Court Justice William H. Rehnquist dissented in three of the cases above, basing his decisions on the belief that the earlier cases—used by the Supreme Court as precedents to justify its decisions in *Schaumburg, Munson,* and *Riley*—involved the dissemination of information and advocacy. But it seems to me that none of these facts were present in the *Schaumburg, Munson,* and *Riley* cases and certainly were not present in the *Madigan* case. (Rehnquist was not on the bench in the *Madigan* case, but his reasoning would certainly apply there and in *Schaumburg, Munson,* and *Riley*.)

To repeat: these cases were simply about soliciting money and supervising fundraisers. They did not involve advocacy or the dissemination of information. Moreover, several of the cases, quoted by the Court in the *Schaumburg, Munson,* and *Riley* cases, involved distributing handbills door-to-door and talking about

> Strange as it may seem, the Supreme Court is more interested in protecting the fundraiser than in protecting the donor.

Jehovah's Witnesses, as well as soliciting money. Courts are particularly protective of free speech when religious groups are involved. Religious groups were not involved in *Schaumburg, Munson, Riley,* or *Madigan.*

Rehnquist made this distinction in all of his dissenting opinions. In *Schaumburg,* he said: "While (fundraising) may be worthy of heightened protection when limited to the dissemination of information ... or when designed to propagate religious beliefs ... I believe that a simple request for money lies far from the core protections of the First Amendment as heretofore interpreted." In the *Munson* case, Rehnquist stated: "Even if limitations on the fees charged by professional fundraisers were subjected to heightened scrutiny, however, those limitations serve a number of legitimate and substantial government interests. They ensure that funds solicited from the public for a charitable purpose will not be excessively diverted to private pecuniary gain. In the process they encourage the public to give by allowing the public to give with confidence that money designed for charity will be spent on charitable purposes."

I believe Rehnquist was correct in distinguishing between cases where the charity or fundraiser were advocating a cause or disseminating information, and cases where the issue involved only asking for money. The latter cases are not entitled to free speech protection.

It's time for donors to be aware of these cases, to ask the right questions, and to forge agreements with fundraisers that limit the amount of money they can pocket. The bulk of money raised should go to the charities involved—not to the fundraisers. The Better Business Bureau of New York suggests 35 percent as the proper amount to go to the fundraiser. That seems reasonable. Anything more than that, I believe, would be a fraudulent use of charitable funds unless this fact is told to the donor.

I assume that most donors would agree—if only they knew that the bulk of their contributions aren't always going to the charities of their choice. It's time for donors to learn the truth. ◢

Naomi B. Levine is chair and executive director of NYU's George H. Heyman Jr. Center for Philanthropy and Fundraising and a regular columnist for *Contribute*. Her next column will appear in the November/December issue.

6.1%:
The rise in American donations to philanthropy in 2005 over the previous year.
Source: *2006 Giving USA*

14%:
The increase in corporate giving in 2005 over the previous year, in a survey of 62 large companies by the Committee to Encourage Corporate Philanthropy in New York.

advocate

NAOMI LEVINE

School for Scandal

Fundraisers should be required to take a course in ethics

Senator Nick Spano

For the past several years, Senator Nick Spano of Westchester, Assemblywoman RoAnn Destito, and Assemblyman John McEneny have sought to pass a bill to require most professionals who raise money for charity to take a course in the ethics and laws of fundraising and philanthropy.

That course, as defined by the proposal, would be mandatory for all full-time salaried employees of charities that raise more than $1 million a year. All professional fundraisers and solicitors who make more than $250,000 a year raising money for charities also would have to take the four-hour course, which would include the following:

: the history of philanthropy in the United States and its effect on the American economy and society;

: a study of federal and state laws and a discussion of the work of the Charities Bureau in New York State relating to fundraising and philanthropy;

: a discussion of ethics and how they differ from laws;

: and an overview of recent cases relating to ethics violations in fundraising.

Under the proposal, universities and colleges could teach the course, online or in a classroom, as long as it was approved by the commissioner of education.

For a while this past summer, it looked like the New York Legislature would finally pass this bill. But then, to the surprise of many, several nonprofit organizations—including the Nonprofit Coordinating Committee of New York, the American Heart Association, and the American Cancer Society—lobbied extensively in Albany to kill the bill. It worked. The proposal, once again this year, was defeated.

Opponents used three arguments to sink the bill:

1 **Affordability.** Critics said the bill would oblige nonprofits to pay for the ethics schooling of their employees, and that would take money away from the needy and others served by the nonprofits. Critics also said the course would take valuable time away from the business of raising money.

2 **Effectiveness.** Opponents asked whether a four-hour ethics course would be enough to make somebody already prone to cutting corners less likely to do so.

3 **Price.** Because only a few organizations and institutions would offer such an ethics course, it was argued, instructors would be tempted to charge top dollar in tuition.

But to all of this, I disagree.

While I respect the integrity and wisdom of those who are making these objections, I feel strongly that it is a wrong assumption that the course would be

> The strongest argument for mandated ethics classes is the growing mistrust of donors toward fundraisers. ...Codes of ethics are not enough.

Naomi Levine

10

107

Self-regulation did not work for corporate America; there is no reason to believe it will work in the nonprofit world.

$625,000

What a Bronx charity, formerly known as the Gloria Wise Boys and Girls Club, will repay the city in a legal settlement reached in September—money that donors intended for children and the elderly but which the nonprofit improperly lent to Air America Radio, a network known for its liberal programming.

The New York Times,
September 28, 2006

unaffordable. Keep in mind that the Legislature can set the fees of courses given by public colleges and universities, thereby keeping them affordable and preventing price hikes—as has been the case with other mandated, professional training courses offered in other fields and professions.

Further, I have no doubt that many groups, including the Association of Fundraising Professionals and the Nonprofit Coordinating Committee of New York, would offer ethics courses, which would, at least, keep prices competitive.

And not everyone would seek reimbursement from their employers, so it's hard to argue that nonprofit budgets would be strained because of such courses. Quite the contrary: Basic training in fundraising laws and ethics would be a kind of preventative medicine, helping nonprofits avoid potentially more costly missteps down the road.

But the strongest argument for mandatory ethics classes is the growing mistrust of donors toward fundraisers of all stripes. At a time when stories about bad nonprofit management, board negligence, excess salaries, fraudulent telemarketing, and even criminal behavior are making the headlines, now is the best time to start requiring fundraisers to get smarter about the laws and ethics that shape nonprofit work.

More than any other group, fundraisers know that trust and donor confidence is critical to success in their work. Lawyers take ethics courses. So must doctors, accountants, and many service workers, and most of them annually.

Under the Spano-Destito-McEneny legislation, all that would be required is one ethics course, to be taken once in a fundraiser's professional lifetime. "If Americans lose faith in charitable organizations, they will stop giving, and those in need will suffer," said IRS Commissioner Mark Everson at a hearing of the Senate Finance Committee last year. Added Senate Finance Committee Chairman Charles Grassley: "I am troubled that there was little to no criticism from the charitable community about the serious problems at American University and the Getty Foundation. Charitable leaders must be a strong voice in condemning inappropriate behavior in their sector."

I couldn't agree more. Not only has the charitable community and its leaders failed to condemn inappropriate behavior, they have only meekly support-

ed federal legislation to tighten the regulation of nonprofits. Charity leaders also opposed a move by 17 attorneys general some years back to sue a telemarketing outfit for fraud because it kept $6 million of the $7 million it collected for a Vietnam veterans group. Charity leaders also have objected to proposals to require ethics courses for fundraisers.

While I believe that most fundraisers are honest, hardworking, committed, and trustworthy human beings, even the "good guys" need education about the evolving nature and challenges of their work if they are to continue to be effective.

Senator Spano, Assemblywoman Destito, and Assemblyman McEneny deserve our thanks for trying to get such legislation passed year after year.

They understand that in this post-Enron era, the nonprofit world is not immune from the shameful and scandalous behavior that has recently plagued corporate America. Unfortunately, the corporations did not and cannot police themselves.

The same could be said of nonprofits. Codes of ethics aren't enough. Self-regulation did not work for corporate America; there is no reason to believe it will work in the nonprofit world.

And if the states do not move in the direction of the Spano-Destito-McEneny bill, I suspect that, having read the Senate Finance Committee report on this issue, Congress will—and perhaps more dramatically.

In recent months, there has been talk in Albany and among those in the fundraising community that Spano might have better luck next year if his bill were to propose making an ethics course voluntary. There is also talk that waiving a portion of the course cost might also make the bill a bit more palatable the next time around.

While I would prefer an ethics course requirement, voluntary coursework is better than nothing at all.

Our profession, however, cannot afford to do any less. ◢

Naomi Levine is chair and executive director of New York University's George H. Heyman, Jr., Center for Philanthropy and Fundraising and teaches a course on fundraising ethics and the law at NYU. Ms. Levine's next column for the magazine will appear in the February/March issue. Please send comments about this column to editors@contributemedia.com.

advocate
NAOMI B. LEVINE

Split Intentions

Private foundations need to walk the talk on their investments

How can a foundation—one created to ease social ills—justify turning a blind eye to the socially irresponsible behavior of the companies in which it invests?

Naomi B. Levine

Bill and Melinda Gates rightly received a groundswell of public accolades and applause from people inside and out of the philanthropy world when they created their private foundation in 2000. Who could say anything negative about a couple donating roughly $30 billion of their own wealth to a foundation created to eradicate global disease, illiteracy, and poverty around the world?

Yet findings by the *Los Angeles Times* earlier this year that the Bill & Melinda Gates Foundation has invested its assets in corporations that contribute to some of the same problems it aims to alleviate are troubling, indeed. The newspaper series raises critical but long overdue questions about how today's new surge of private mega-foundations, essentially the largely unaccountable new philanthropic vehicles of the newly wealthy, are being run and managed.

What should be the investment guidelines of a foundation? Should getting the best "dollar return" on its investments be the only goal? Or should a foundation also consider the social responsibility of the companies in which it invests?

The answer, to me at least, is simple: a foundation, dedicated to improving the world we live in, should invest its money in companies that share its concerns. Of course, one might argue that a corporation owes its shareholders maximum investment returns and so may need to ignore social responsibility, although the trend today is in the opposite direction. But how can a foundation—one created to ease social ills—justify turning a blind eye to the socially irresponsible behavior of the companies in which it invests?

These are not new questions. But as the number of new mega-foundations grow in number and clout, these questions cannot now—in my view—be raised often enough.

Consider what the Gates Foundation has been doing: the *Los Angeles Times* series reported the foundation is spending millions of dollars worldwide funding inoculations to protect health, including in the Niger Delta. Yet at the same time, it has invested in the Italian petroleum company, Eni. The Eni company is one of several with plants in the delta that pollutes the air with flares of oil containing up to 250 toxic chemicals, many of which "have caused an epidemic of bronchitis in adults and asthma and blurred vision in children," the newspaper says. The paper also says the foundation is additionally invested in Royal Dutch Shell, Exxon Mobil Corporation, Chevron Corporation, and Total of France—companies responsible, along with Eni, for most of the flares blanketing the delta with pollution at levels above those permitted in the United States and Europe.

Also according to the series, the Gates Founda-

ILLUSTRATION: DANIEL BEJAR

The Bill & Melinda Gates Foundation has invested its assets in many corporations whose behavior contributes to the very problems their foundation aims to alleviate in the world.

tion's investments, totaling at least $8.7 billion—or 41% of its assets, not including U.S. and foreign government securities—have been in companies "that countered the foundation's charitable goals or socially concerned philosophy." The foundation donates 5% of its assets every year and invests the other 95%.

Much of the Gates Foundation's investments are in companies that "have failed tests of social responsibility because of environmental lapses, employment discrimination, disregard for workers' rights, or unethical behavior," the newspaper said. These include: pharmaceutical companies that have restricted the flow of key medicines to poor people in developing nations; mortgage companies that have been accused in lawsuits or by government officials of making it easier for thousands of people to lose their homes; a healthcare company with a history of scandal, lawsuits, federal raids for Medicare fraud, kickbacks, and poor and dangerous patient care; companies ranked among the worst U.S. and Canadian air polluters; and four large chocolate makers, which buy their cocoa from West Africa, where, according to a report from the International Institute for Tropical Agriculture, a group supported by the U.S. Agency for International Development, 284,000 children—many younger than 14—work under hazardous conditions.

Even more disturbing, though, is the fact that the Gates Foundation has not used its considerable financial clout to influence companies to change their policies. Several other major foundations—most of them older mega-foundations outside the realm of today's "new donors," such as the Ford, MacArthur, Rockefeller, Nathan Cumming, and Charles Stewart Mott foundations, have not only developed investment guidelines that support their missions, but also participate directly in shareholder initiatives, voting their proxies to influence corporate behavior.

Gates Foundation officials, however, in a statement following the *Los Angeles Times* investigation, made it clear the foundation does "not get involved in proxy issues." And when Gates Foundation President Patty Stonesifer was asked to comment about this, *The Economist* magazine reported that she brushed aside the issue as one that "certainly can provoke an interesting debate." She further explained

this in a letter to the *Los Angeles Times*. "Changes in our investment practice would have little or no impact on the suffering identified in the *Los Angeles Times* article(s)," she wrote. "The foundation does not own big-enough stakes in companies to influence their behavior through shareholder activism—even if it does nod to political correctness by declining to invest in cigarette firms." A far better way to help people, she said, "is by making grants and working with other donors to improve health, reduce poverty, and strengthen education." She repeated that point at a recent gathering at the New York Public Library.

In my view, Stonesifer is too smart to believe that the foundation's corporate investments should play no role in furthering its program goals; the foundation's poor example here should be a siren call for reforms and stepped-up oversight.

"Foundations are stewards of wealth for the benefit of society—and receive tax advantages on that basis," writes Joel Fleishman, professor of law and public policy at Duke University, in his new book, *The Foundation: A Great American Secret*. Foundations have, in other words, an obligation to foster the public good.

Paul Hawken, an expert on socially beneficial investing who directs the Natural Capital Institute, said recently: "(The) dirty secret of many large philanthropies (is that) foundations donate to groups trying to heal the future, but with their investments they steal from the future."

The *Los Angeles Times* deserves a special accolade for its findings and also for causing the foundation community to start talking about its investment policies. If foundations, whose assets now total more than $200 billion, begin to use their investment strength to influence corporate behavior, the *Los Angeles Times* will have performed a great service to the world of philanthropy and to the global community of which we are so important a part. ◢

Naomi B. Levine is chair and executive director of New York University's Heyman Center for Philanthropy and Fundraising and a regular columnist for *Contribute*. E-mail comments to editors@contributemedia.com

13

advocate
NAOMI B. LEVINE

Poverty 101
Overseas giving by Americans is on the rise, but does it matter?

These young people brave heat, disease, bad food, and even civil war.

Naomi B. Levine

In larger numbers than ever, college students want to study abroad: more than 200,000 American students are flocking to foreign universities each year, an increase of nearly 150 percent over the last decade. Thousands are enrolled in global philanthropy courses, and as part of their studies, they are working for organizations involved in global projects created by American foundations, corporations, and donors at home and abroad.

These young advocates are prepared to work, often in dire circumstances and in some of the poorest countries in the world. They brave heat, disease, bad food, and even civil war. They take seriously the value of helping those less fortunate, sentiments expressed recently by Bill Gates to Harvard's 2007 graduates. Gates urged students to work "to reduce (global) inequities," to be "activists," and to help people living in "unspeakable" poverty and disease. He

urged students to "start sooner" to help those in need and to "carry on longer."

Listening to students in NYU's philanthropy classes, it's clear that Mr. Gates' sentiments carried resonance. These students want to volunteer overseas and they're urging the organizations for which they work to contribute more financially to global philanthropy. They, too, are making such gifts.

And they're not the only ones. Giving USA says giving by Americans to international affairs organizations is rising—up by an average of 16.3 percent since 1987, with 12.5 percent of that in the last 10 years, alone. That's a higher boost than that logged by many domestic causes—and 1.6 percent more than giving to the environment.

Dollar-wise, $11.34 billion was given to international affairs organizations in 2006. Several mega-gifts helped, such as the $50 million that Warren Buffet gave to the Nuclear Threat Initiative, the $50 million given by George Soros to help eliminate poverty in Africa, and the $225 million given by David Rockefeller to the Rockefeller Brothers fund, to create a global development fund to address challenges to poverty, healthcare, global economy, and international trade. President Clinton's global initiative pours millions into international aid. And these tallies don't count microfinancing aid, through which Americans and others extend small loans to people around the world too poor to qualify for bank loans.

But is it enough? Can it ever be enough? Several students involved in overseas projects have come back from their stints abroad both disillusioned and heartsick. Problems facing the needy abroad are so overwhelming, they say, that the work of philanthropists and advocates is, ultimately, of miniscule value—just a "Band-Aid" for countries bleeding to death by civil war, political corruption, and rampant, ethnic rivalries.

These are not just the cries of inexperienced, overzealous idealists. A handful of recent books and studies also suggest that foreign aid is sometimes oversold, including the superb new book, *The Bottom Billion*, by Paul Collier, the World Bank's former research economist and the director for the Study of African Economies at Oxford University.

Collier states that people in rich countries approach Africa's problems with more emotion than empirical evidence, and while philanthropy and generous contributions are important, Collier says the problems in these countries are so extreme that only governments can really solve them. Philanthropy, he concludes, cannot cope with the civil wars, the political corruption, and the social and economic problems that plague these countries. "Civil war, it turns out, has nothing much to do with the legacy of colonialism or income inequality or the political oppression of minorities," Collier writes. "Three things turn out to increase the risk of conflict: the relatively high proportion of young uneducated men; an imbalance between ethnic groups and one tending to outnumber the rest; and the supply of natural resources like diamonds and oil, which simultaneously encourage and help finance the rebellions."

Collier isn't alone in questioning the impact of foreign aid. Writing in *The New York Times* recently, columnist Nicholas D. Kristof cites a study by two former International Monetary Fund economists, Raghuram Rajan and Arvind Subramanian, who say there is "little robust evidence of a positive (or negative) relationship between aid inflows into a country and its economic growth." Kristof, quoting from an upcoming article by the pair in *The Review of Economics and Statistics*, says they found "no evidence that aid works better in better policy or geographical environments, or that certain forms of aid work better than others. ...For aid to be effective in the future, the aid apparatus will have to be rethought."

Even microfinancing has begun to take a hit from some economists. In a recent article in the *Stanford Social Innovation Review*, strategy professor Aneel Karnani says that while microcredit is "the newest silver bullet for alleviating poverty," has "attracted untold billions of dollars," and "earned Muhammad Yunus a Nobel Prize," it does not significantly alleviate poverty. "Microloans," Karnani says, "are more beneficial to borrowers living above the poverty line than to borrowers living below it: people with more income are willing to take the risks most likely to increase income. Poor borrowers, on the other hand, tend to take out conservative loans and rarely invest in new technology, fixed capital, or hiring of labor." Therefore, governments, businesses, and civil society, Karnani says, "would be well-advised to reallocate their resources and energies away from microfinance and into supporting larger enterprises in labor intensive industries" — much as China does. Governments, businesses and civic leaders also should provide basic services to improve the employability and productivity of the poor, Karnani says. Otherwise, he says, these leaders "will miss the mark of lifting people out of poverty."

So does all of this mean we should give up on foreign aid? Can philanthropy help solve the world's ills, or will it always fall short in the absence of good government and innovative thinking?

The disillusionment of many young people is based on real problems and, to be sure, philanthropy cannot, by itself, solve them. Foreign-aid philanthropy has never been enough, in and of itself.

But it is equally important for young people to keep in mind that caught in the terrible crises of these countries are individuals—innocent men, women, and children. To provide them with food, medicine, and a roof over their heads is of tremendous value, and shall always be of tremendous value, even if such types of help offer no ultimate solution to the chronic problems causing poverty around the world.

Take note, then, young advocates: Do not let the overriding political, ethnic, and economic problems of the world snuff out your desire to help and encourage philanthropic aid to poor countries. Yes, philanthropy to those in need overseas may, indeed, be a "Band-Aid." But even this type of giving can make a vast difference to those who suffer while the rest of us wait for, and create, longer-range solutions. ◢

Naomi B. Levine is chair and executive director of New York University's Heyman Center for Philanthropy and Fundraising and a regular columnist for *Contribute*.

> ## Philanthropy, alone, cannot cope with the civil wars, political corruption and social and economic problems that plague these countries.

16.3%
The rise since 1987 in philanthropic giving to international affairs organizations, with 12.5 percent of that increase occurring since 1997.
Giving USA 2006

980 million
The so-called "bottom billion"—the number of people who populate the poorest one-sixth of the world's population, of which 70 percent live in Africa.
Economist Paul Collier, in his new book, *The Bottom Billion: Why the Poorest Countries are Failing and What Can Be Done.*

advocate
NAOMI B. LEVINE AND CLAIRE L. GAUDIANI

Classwork

Fundraisers should be trained and licensed to serve

Today, women own 51% of America's individual wealth.

These are, as our NYU colleague Paul Light, of the Wagner School, has said recently, "times that try nonprofit souls." Add fundraisers' souls to the list.

Globalization, social engineering, microfinance, metric evaluation, younger and more hands-on philanthropists, increased planned giving, new levels of diversity, talk of regulation, crisis management, billion-dollar mega-giving—all of these things are bringing new words, demands, approaches, and problems to the work of the philanthropic fundraiser that have rarely or only occasionally been confronted in the past.

In the past five years, more than 6,000 students have taken courses in fundraising at the Heyman Center here in New York. Around the country, thousands more are taking such courses. Since fundraising existed long before such classwork appeared on the horizon to professionalize it all, perhaps it's appropriate to ask: Are such courses really needed? Are nonprofit fundraising certification and Master's degrees necessary?

There is no question. Such professionalization is needed as never before, and here's why: Since 1990, the number of social profit organizations in this country has grown, at a clip of some 20 percent per year. There are now more than 1.8 million nonprofit and social profit organizations on the scene today.

In 1990, these institutions controlled $2 trillion; the nearly 2 million organizations today control nearly $4 trillion. Despite that number, they all need funding; strong and well-run boards; well-organized programs; clarity of mission, vision and ethics; and smart ways to measure their own effectiveness.

Moreover, they all need money and are competing against each other for it as never before. Rivalry to raise ever-more financial support just to keep these organizations afloat keeps intensifying. Moreover, the job of fundraising, itself, has gotten harder, demanding far more knowledge and skill to perform well.

Consider planned giving. This form of contribution was always something an effective fundraiser needed to know a bit about. But today, with more than 31 percent of gifts to charities involving some form of planning—such as bequests, pooled income, remainder and charitable lead trusts, to name just a few—fundraisers now have to be tax whizzes—and financial brainiacs, to boot. More than 2.2 million Web sites now offer input on wealth transfer planning. Philanthropy holds a critically important place in estate planning if advisers are well prepared to make a space for it in their work with clients. Fundraisers for social profit groups, to be successful, must have more knowledge of federal and state tax laws and greater

ILLUSTRATION: EDEL RODRIGUEZ

Donors are different now: they have many more opportunities to contribute to more causes in more ways than ever before...Financial advisers must meet significant requirements to qualify for practice, but fundraisers don't—and we should.

knowledge of the legal aspects of fundraising.

But that's not all. Consider diversity issues. There were always concerns about the generally low levels of racial diversity in the sector, but today, the lack of greater diversity among fundraising professionals and nonprofit leaders presents an ever-greater concern. America is now far more diverse than ever before, yet many nonprofit boards don't reflect the upsurge. But unless these boards become less insular from those they serve, fundraising will become harder and more expensive.

Change in the sector also is about behavior. Donors are different now: they have many more opportunities to contribute to more causes in more ways than ever before. Online giving is as easy as online trading. Donors are now more savvy about their options, more personally engaged with recipients. And with the awesome complexity of the financial services industries, professionals in philanthropy—just like financial advisers and investment managers—need to add real value to the more heavily risk-sensitive decisions that donors to charities make. Financial advisers and investment managers must meet significant requirements to qualify for practice. Fundraisers don't, and we should.

And consider gender. Women have always played a key role in fundraising, as far back as 1641, when Lady Moulson gave the first scholarship to Harvard. Yet today, women's involvement is extraordinary, not only as donors and volunteers, but also as professionals. Today, women own 51 percent of the country's wealth. Many are working in high-paid positions. Some are even the heads of Fortune 500 companies. Moreover, they are inheriting large amounts of money. In the next five years, those numbers will be tremendous. Will they bring a different approach to

$4 trillion

The amount of wealth controlled by the nearly 2 million nonprofit and social profit institutions in America today.

Claire Gaudiani, NYU Heyman Center for Philanthropy and Fundraising

philanthropy? Are gender issues really critical? Will female philanthropists be giving to different types of organizations? And must fundraisers learn to solicit women differently than men?

And what about the so-called "new philanthropist" among younger donors of both sexes? Are donors who bring high income and demands for greater effectiveness and faster results forcing changes in how fundraisers must solicit money?

These issues, of course, join a list of others now on the plate of today's fundraisers—right up there along with concerns about ethics, board governance, and calls by lawmakers on the federal and state levels for greater oversight of nonprofits in general. Is self-regulation of nonprofits and other social profit organizations enough? Should all fundraisers be required to take at least one course in the law and the ethics of fundraising, mandated and approved by the state? And should portions of the Sarbanes-Oxley law be applied to nonprofit organizations?

If fundraising is to be viewed today as a profession and not merely be all about selling cookies for the Girl Scouts, courses—especially those given within colleges and universities—are critical.

Today's times demand it; those in need of what social profit organizations have to offer deserve it. There is much work to be done and no more time to lose. ◢

Naomi B. Levine

Claire L. Gaudiani

Naomi B. Levine is chair and executive director of New York University's Heyman Center for Philanthropy and Fundraising and a regular columnist for CONTRIBUTE. Claire L. Gaudiani is a professor at the center and an expert in the history of American philanthropy and author of *The Greater Good: How Philanthropy Drives the American Economy and Can Save Capitalism.*

The Princeton Case: Money-Money-Money

Nothing intrigues the media as much as a David and Goliath story, i.e., an underdog, puny and ill equipped, fighting in the name of justice against a giant behemoth monster. The current lawsuit brought by William Robertson, and members of the Robertson family and friends, against Princeton University has been cast in such a light with the Robertsons as the little underdogs against the giant $16 billion dollar endowed Princeton. (Most of the Robertsons are far from being puny underdogs, with William Robertson, a major heir of the A & P fortune.)

The Robertsons and their lawyers have, moreover, cast the issue as one involving "donor rights" – arguing that Princeton has ignored the purposes of the original grant. They have done this so effectively that most newspapers and magazines have referred to the case as the "most important case in higher education over the question of honoring the wishes of the donor."

I do not believe the issue is donor's rights, but rather an interpretation of the language that accompanied the gift. In none of the papers filed has Princeton denied that the donor has "rights." On the contrary, it believes it has in the past and is today carrying out the donor's wishes. The Robertsons disagree. They believe the grant should be read in the narrowest fashion—with Princeton reading it in broad terms, which it believes conforms more accurately to the academic requirements needed to meet the donor's mission.

I repeat: in none of its papers does Princeton deny its obligation to meet donor's intent. Put differently, the issue is "interpretation" of a donor's document—not the "rights" of the donor. The latter is a "given" in today's philanthropic world and does not need a law suit to confirm that.

Specifically, the facts of the case are as follows:
In 1961, the donor, Marie Robertson, the heir to the A&P fortune, granted 700,000 shares of A&P stock, worth at that time $35 million dollars. This stock has funded an endowment worth today approximately $880 million. The foundation was to be run by seven trustees; four appointed by Princeton and three by the Robertson family.

The Foundation Certificate of Incorporation authorized the Foundation to pay the income on this capital to Princeton University, to support a graduate school, at Princeton, as part of its Woodrow Wilson School for the purposes of strengthening the government of the United States by maintaining a program where men and women could be educated and trained for government service—with emphasis on training for government service careers in international affairs. The grant was also to provide scholarships and fellowships in this area and for collateral and auxiliary services, and programs "in furtherance of the object and purpose of the grant."

The plaintiffs claim that the language of this incorporation certificate requires Princeton to use the Robertson money to support only courses in international affairs and only faculty that teach these courses within the Graduate School in the Woodrow Wilson School. It contends further that few graduates of this program now work in government services in the international arena and that the program is not a distinguished one.

Princeton claims that such a reading would make the Graduate School within the Woodrow Wilson School a "vocational school"—the antithesis of what a Princeton education stands for. It believes that to be equipped to work in international affairs requires an understanding of politics, economics, the social problems we face as a nation, as well as an understanding of global issues. International affairs, Princeton states, are so interrelated with domestic affairs that the two should not and could not be separated. To understand what the United States is doing abroad, in other words, one has to understand the economic, sociological and political issues the U.S. faces at home.

"There are few domestic issues without international implications and events abroad quickly make themselves felt internationally."

"The Woodrow Wilson School is not an island unto itself at Princeton. Teaching, research, and publication at this School cuts across the traditional academic fields and so it is in a sense interdisciplinary."

The Certificate of Incorporation, Princeton points out, also states that the men and women enrolled in the graduate program may prepare themselves for careers in government service in international affairs. The use of the word "may" indicates that some students may enroll to take advantage of the School's public policy program for careers in government service—not restricted to international affairs. In brief, Princeton reads the grant as providing an opportunity for students to prepare for "responsibility in public and international affairs and not restricted to international affairs only.

For all of these reasons, Princeton used the Robertson grant money for faculty in various departments of the University—to provide the interdisciplinary framework for this program. I share with Princeton its belief that such a program should be interdisciplinary and the decision of what should be included in the education of men and women for government and international affairs must be an academic decision and not the responsibility of lawyers, or the heirs of the grantor or the Supreme Court of New Jersey.

Does the language in the grant from the Robertsons preclude this? I can see nothing in any of the documents creating the foundation, or in any subsequent memorandum including reports to the Foundation Board, that prohibits such a conclusion. Indeed, everything in such documents encourages a broad interpretation of the Foundation's mission, which from an academic point of view makes good sense.

"From the earliest days of the Robertson Foundation, the School had pursued this mandate by choosing students dedicated to public service and providing a rigorous multidisciplinary training that enables them to become leaders in government."

The University's press release announcing this gift and minutes of the Foundation board when the gift was first accepted also stress the fact that the gift was "designed to prepare personnel for careers in public and international affairs. None of this was kept secret from the board.

Princeton also pointed out that after the Vietnam War and Watergate it was harder to get young people to go straight into government, and many students did go "into a more mobile career, moving back and forth, in and out of government service and private companies which did government work."

The Woodrow Wilson School, however, continued "to encourage students to enter public service in the government and multilateral agencies" and constantly examined its faculty and curriculum to make certain the School produced "not only top-quality leaders, but also approaches and answers to the problems facing these students." All of these discussions were held at board meetings and I can see no secrecy involved in these decisions about the directions the School was taking. But again, documents can be read differently and the final interpretation will be in the judge's hands.

As for the quality of the Woodrow Wilson School, the plaintiff is on very weak ground. The School's reputation continues to be one of academic excellence with few peers that surpass it.

Having said all this, I believe all of these issues are ancillary. The main reason for this lawsuit is the fact that in the early summer of 2002 the Finance Committee of the Robertson Foundation recommended that Princo, the University's investment company, manage the foundation's assets—not the Investment Committee on which Mr. Robertson sat. At that point, Mr. Robertson threatened to sue. He did, in fact, sue a few weeks after this 2002 vote to explore other potential management firms.

Subsequently, two members of the Investment Committee voted with the board to consider potential firms other than Princo. Apparently, no such firm was satisfactory and the foundation board eventually voted four to three to retain Princo subject to the continued oversight of the Investment Committee and the Robertson Foundation Board.

It was that act of hiring Princo that prompted the family designated trustees to file a complaint, claiming that transferring the money to Princo was a violation of the Certificate of Incorporation of the Foundation. This was the major issue in the

original complaint. Indeed, in the summary request to the judge in this complaint, the first issue the plaintiff listed was a request that the judge stop Princeton from "ending control and management of the assets of the foundation to Princo" and stop the commingling of the assets of the foundation with the Princeton endowment. On these issues, the Court has spoken. It believes the University had the right to retain Princo, and that the plaintiff's arguments that retaining Princo would violate donor intent was "baseless."

However, the question of whether Princeton really searched for an alternative to Princo as a management firm, and on the question of commingling, the court rejected Princeton's request for summary judgment, believing that the facts need further exploration—which will occur when the case comes up for a trial. I repeat: the first complaint that started this suit was largely based on the transfer of the management of the Robertson's Foundation investment policy to Princo.

There are many other issues of mismanagement, inadequate reporting, and disclosure the plaintiffs have raised. On the evidence submitted so far, it is difficult to tell how these aspects of the case will be decided. Princeton has already reimbursed the Robertson Foundation $782,375 for "inadequate disclosure."

And even before a final decision is handed down on the other issues by Judge Neil H. Shuster, who already has ruled out a jury trial, the plaintiffs have been calling other Universities to see if they would accept scholarships in accordance with the Robertson mission. Princeton claims the Certificate of Incorporation of the Foundation states unambiguously that only Princeton can benefit from the grant. Judge Shuster has made clear that he will sever Princeton's relationship with the Foundation only if he finds "the most egregious and nefarious of circumstances." He did not rule out that possibility. He clearly wants to keep the options open.

It is now five years since the case began. Hopefully, in the next year or two it will finally be tried. The legal fees alone have amounted to more than $20 million each for both the plaintiffs and the defendants.

When all is said and done, I believe, the real issue comes down to money. A concern with donor's rights sounds less crass than a concern with money. But anyone who has taken the time to read the thousands of pages of complaints, memorandum, and court decisions on both sides of this case (which I believe the press has not done), will come to the conclusion that if the plaintiffs—especially William Robertson—did not want more control over the Foundation funds and was not opposed to transferring control of the money to Princeton, the case would never have been brought.

But regardless of how the court decides these issues, the case has one important lesson where donors are concerned. It demonstrates the importance of writing a clear gift agreement with language that states without ambiguity the donor's intent. If this case underscores this lesson for donors and their lawyers, it will be well worth the $20 million each of the parties have spent. ◆

Conflict of Interest

On Thursday, October 11, 2007 the *New York Times* had a story with the headline: "Chairman's Son-in-Law Hired as Architect for Carnegie Expansion." The story reported that the Board of Carnegie Hall hired Mr. Bibliowicz, the son-in-law of its chairman, Sandy Weill, as the architect for Carnegie Hall's $150 million expansion.

Carnegie officials said: "They were impressed by a previous project by his firm—the design of the well-regarded home of the Alvin Ailey American Dance Theater." I am sure these officials of Carnegie Hall were also impressed by the fact that the chairwoman of Alvin Ailey is Mr. Bibliowicz' mother-in-law, Joan Weill, and that she has been a major contributor to Alvin Ailey. I have a suspicion, too, that the fact that Mr. Weill had given $50 million to Carnegie Hall also impressed the Carnegie Hall officials as much as or more than the architectural design submitted by Mr. Weill's son-in-law.

Keep in mind that the Board of Carnegie Hall consists of some of the most distinguished and important philanthropists, including Mercedes T. Bass; John Rosenwald, Jr.; James Wolfensohn; Clarissa Alcott Bronfman; and Felix G. Rohatyn, to mention a few of its more than 50 Board members. And the Board of the Alvin Ailey Dance Foundation consists of a similar array of important, knowledgeable philanthropists.

It is hard to believe that such a sophisticated group was unaware of the many stories in the press—many first-page stories—about conflict of interest and self-dealings. These stories, plus the hearings of the Senate Finance Committee on Non-Profits, the statements of the Senate Committee's Chairman, Senator Chuck Grassley, the codes of the Better Business Bureau and other associations of non-profit organizations, and the scores of articles on conflict of interest have all made clear that not only must organizations—profit and non-profit—have conflict of interest statements, but that these statements must be interpreted and implemented in a fashion that keeps an arm's length distance between donors and the institution. And any transactions that bring personal or professional gain to a donor or his or her family must be avoided.

The case of the Nature Conservancy is a dramatic example of how one of the nation's largest and respectable non-profit organizations became the subject of a critical series of articles in the *Washington Post* for ignoring these rules. The *Post* revealed that the Nature Conservancy made some unusual land arrangements with donors, many of them board members. The Nature Conservancy would, for example purchase a tract of land to keep it from development. It might pay $1 million for it. It would then put a "conservation easement" on it—a restriction to prevent the owner from developing it.

The Nature Conservancy would then sell the land for $700,000 with the easement, because the easement reduces its value. Frequently, the purchaser would then give the Nature Conservancy a gift of $300,000 to make up the difference, getting an appropriate tax benefit. There was nothing illegal in this transaction—except that the *Post* discovered that many of the purchasers of these land deals were trustees of the Nature Conservancy. The *Post* characterized this as inside dealing. The Nature Conservancy became subjected to an examination by the Senate Finance Committee, which cast a veil of suspicion upon the Conservancy. After months of investigation and harmful publicity, the Nature Conservancy adopted a policy that prohibited the purchase of land by any of its board members and their immediate families.

Hiring the son-in-law of the chairman of your Board, who is also your major donor, of course, is factually different than the land deal of the Nature Conservancy. It is the same, however, in that it involves inside dealings which the Senate Finance Committee frowned upon as an unethical conflict of interest. In both cases the institutions were not keeping an "arm's length distance" between the donor and the institution and the inside dealing clearly brought a professional gain to a donor or a member of the donor's family.

To say as Clive Gillinson, Carnegie Hall's Executive and Artistic Director, said: "You can't disqualify someone because they're somebody's son-in-law," misses the point. Mr. Bibliowicz was not just "somebody's son-in-law." He is the son-in-law of the most powerful member of the institution's Board. He in the son-in-law of Sandy Weill—its chairman!

Mr. Weill, for his part, has been very open about this, saying unequivocally that he had nothing to do with his son-in-law, Mr. Bibliowicz' selection; he played no role in the process; and he excused himself from the meetings when his son-in-law's hiring was discussed. On the other hand, it is reported in the *Times* that there was "no formal competition." Apparently, another proposal had come in from another architectural firm, but Mr. Bibliowicz' design was viewed as "superior."

The story also said that Mrs. Weill had recommended her son-in-law originally as a volunteer to come up with a new design for the Alvin Ailey $56 million new home on 55th Street and Ninth Avenue. The Board ultimately chose Mr. Bibliowicz because of his "volunteer work and design." Mrs. Weill states that she had nothing to do with his selection. The fact that Mr. Bibliowicz had only modest experience in designing performing arts spaces before that commission apparently did not deter the Board from giving him this assignment.

I have no doubt that Mr. and Mrs. Weill were stating the truth when they said that they did not overtly pressure the Boards at Carnegie Hall and Alvin Ailey to accept Mr. Bibliowicz. It is equally true that the Boards were kept informed of Mr. Bibliowicz' hiring and as stated above, Mr. Weill excused himself when the issue was raised. Transparency and disclosure were never in doubt.

But it is incredulous to believe that the Boards were not influenced by the $50 million that Mr. Weill has given to

Women in Philanthropy

Will they change the direction of philanthropy? Is their approach to philanthropy different from that of men?

One of the most talked about aspects of philanthropy today is the increasing importance of women in philanthropy—as fundraisers, foundation executives and donors. The latter are of special interest today, as women now own 51% of the country's wealth and 65% of the stock traded on the stock exchange every day. They also own 6.2 million businesses; they have high powered jobs and high salaries in corporate America and are expected to inherit billions of dollars in the next five decades.

From the time our country was formed, women have always been involved in philanthropy. The first scholarship in America was given to Harvard by a woman, Lady Moulson, in 1641. Throughout our history women have given generously of their time and money to help "the poor and the orphans," to establish women's colleges; to support education, the arts, churches, medicine, and scores of social programs. The difference today is that the number of women involved in philanthropy and the extent of their wealth has increased dramatically. And while the women in the past generally were shy about publicly announcing their gifts (as a concern with money was not ladylike), that is hardly the mantra of today's woman.

In short, the gender gap in philanthropy in giving money, publicizing such gifts, and exerting the power that money provides is closing. Indeed, in some cases it may have already closed.
Yes, there are still more men sitting on the boards of prestigious non-profits. Yes, more men are still giving larger gifts than women of comparable wealth. And yes, many women are still not as knowledgeable as men on the use of tax benefits in the design and formation of large gifts. But here, too, the scene is changing. More women now sit on boards; the size of their gifts is increasing; and many have financial acumen—certainly those who are working and earning their own money.

The big questions today are: how will the increase in women's giving affect philanthropy? Do women give differently than men? Are they more concerned with social issues? Are they more emotionally involved in the organizations and projects they support? Are the recipients of their gifts different than the non-profits that are supported by male donors? Research in this field is still in its early stages and the results are often conflicting. A recent study says: "Indeed, much of what has been published in the last decade—research as well as journalism—misinterprets the scant survey data available, recycles stereotypes, and generalizes inappropriately from anecdotes and case studies." I share those concerns.

Keeping that in mind, it is interesting to note that most of the books and articles that have recently been published about women's philanthropy take the position that women bring a voice in philanthropy that is different than their male counterparts; that women want change and creativity in philanthropy; they want to emotionally connect to the organizations they support; they want new solutions to old problems; they want to be involved before they make their gifts, and they give to different organizations than men.

I do not agree with these conclusions. While, obviously, there are differences between men and women, I do not believe these differences play out in any significant fashion in philanthropy. I have found that male donors also want to make change; they want creative and new solutions to problems; they want to give to innovative and cutting edge programs; they want to be involved in the projects they support; and many are emotionally committed to the causes to which they make their gifts, and both groups give largely to education, medicine, religious institutions, the arts and social programs. Women's funds, however, do restrict their gifts to women's and children's causes. But these funds, by and large, represent only a small portion of philanthropy gifts.

Indeed, the new "young philanthropists" in all the articles being written about them—many of whom are men—make it very clear that they insist on being part of the projects they support. They want to know how their money is spent; they want to use business methods to evaluate the effectiveness of their giving; and they want to support innovative ideas—not simply the status quo. Many of their projects and programs are aimed at "improving the world," providing food for the hungry, medicine for the sick, homes for the homeless and myriad projects that they hope will provide a safety net for the underprivileged. These projects represent the donors' deep social concerns. I repeat: there are as many men in these programs as there are women.

One final note, keep in mind that the election of women as heads of government—Indira Gandhi in India, Golda Meir in Israel, and Margaret Thatcher in England—in no way added a warmer, more emotional or human attitude toward social problems or war. Indeed, the opposite could be said of each of them. This merely underscores my belief that gender does not necessarily play a definitive role in changing perspectives or priorities in government, business, or the non-profits. ◆

The Miracle of New York University: A Case Study

How Presidents, Boards, and Academic Leadership Committed to Fundraising Remade a Bankrupt University Into a World-Class Educational Institution

Introduction

The 60s and 70s were bitter times for NYU. The University was close to bankruptcy. Its budget was continuously in deficit. At one point it had funds sufficient only for a three month operation and it had a debt of $40 million. The situation was so bad that the clerical staff and faculty were asked to voluntarily take a cut in their salaries. Competition from other colleges and universities was severe especially with the announcement of open enrollment by City University. Academic standards were modest. Many alumni were bitter and disillusioned when the University sold its beloved Heights campus in 1973. Fundraising was dismal. During these years the University raised between $20 million and $30 million a year, which included its Medical Center (school and hospital) and its Law School. The school had few if any dormitories. It was a commuter school with most of its students taking the subway to school every day and living at home. Students from outside NYC were few. There was no recreation center; no central library with books scattered throughout the University in areas that were often airless and badly lit. It was not a university of "first choice" for students or faculty.

And today, just 35 years later, the University is not only fiscally stable, but is recognized as one of the worlds's most acclaimed centers of higher education and research. Students are clamoring to come to NYU; its academic rankings are among the highest, it is raising more than $400 million a year and it completed one of the largest, if not the largest building campaigns in the last decade, which included the construction of a magnificent sports center, a beautiful new student center, six new dormitories, and scores of new laboratories and classrooms.

What produced this miracle? How could a near bankrupt university become a great university with a balanced budget, more applications than it can handle, distinguished faculty, and outstanding fundraising in so short a time? It is that story "as a case study" that this article will present. Hopefully, the lessons and process explained in this case study and the critical role that fundraising played in the University's transformation will be useful to other organizations, large and small, who face problems similar to what NYU faced 35 years ago. So let me repeat: large or small, the process discussed in this article and the rules set forth, are generic, I believe, and are fundamental to any effective fundraising campaign.

History

Before trying to understand how NYU remade itself, it is useful to look at its history during the 60s and 70s. Indeed, as you look at the enormity of the challenges that the University faced in those years, its stunning recovery and growth seems even more remarkable.

First, like most universities throughout the country, NYU during the 60s had its share of student unrest on the campus. This frequently disrupted classes and caused faculty and the administration to spend more time on how to deal with these outbreaks and less time on educational policy.

I have no doubt that these disruptions were partly to blame for the decline in student applications to the University during this period. But there were other problems. The decline in the quality of life in New York City, especially in the Greenwich Village area, the increase in drug sales and crime, and the intense competition for recruitment by City University, with its open enrollment announcement—all of these played important roles in lessening the interest of students to come to NYU and the Greenwich Village area.

And so by the 70s the University was facing impending financial disaster. The crisis, in fact, was so bad that the prospect of bankruptcy was now a very real possibility. President James Hester and the Board of Trustees then made the wrenching decision to sell its much loved University Heights campus. This campus was beautiful. It had magnificent buildings, dormitories, athletic fields, and one of the countries most elegant libraries, Gould Hall, designed by Stanford White. It housed the Undergraduate College of Arts and Science and in this bucolic environment, students, according to Chancellor McCracken, who devised the idea and began its construction in 1895, stated that "The Heights would be where students could enjoy the country environment, and yet be able to study close at hand the great city" *(The Miracle on Washington Square*, Dim & Cricco, Lexington Books (2000) pg. 113).

But, President Hester had no alternative but to sell. If he did not sell, it was clear that the University would have to close. That he faced enormous opposition from students, faculty, and alumni goes without saying. They were outraged, angry, and bitter. They loved the Heights. With its sale many felt their ties to the University were broken. These feelings were so strong that it took several years to overcome. But, as said above, Hester had no choice. The money received from that sale gave the University some breathing time. It paid off its $40 million to creditors and

23

119

it provided help for salaries and scholarships.

But even that money was not enough to keep the University from moving closer and closer to bankruptcy. Financial conditions went from bad to worse. In 1975, a new president John Sawhill was brought in to try to salvage the situation.

Sawhill

Sawhill was not an academic. He was an economist, a PhD graduate from the Stern School of Business, and had a career history in both corporate financial services and management and in government as Director of the Federal Energy Administration.

To achieve the balance in the budget, Sawhill was relentless in cutting costs, in avoiding duplication academically and administratively; consolidating departments where necessary; and most importantly in pressing for the sale of the Muller Company, a pasta factory that NYU's Law School had received through a trust fund. The Law School Foundation acquired this company in 1947 and the income gave the Law School the financial strength—unlike the other schools within the University to become one of the country's leading law schools. Sawhill argued that the Law School would not be viewed as a first rate school if the University went bankrupt. Martin Lipton, then Chair of the Law School Board, and now the Chair of NYU's Board of Trustees, not only agreed with this but took the lead in pushing this forward and urging that a portion of the cash that would be gained by its sale be used to help the University, as well as the Law School. How the money would be divided between the University and the School of Law was hotly debated. Mr. Lipton played a key role in resolving that conflict. The result was that the money was divided between the University and the Law School. The argument that the Law School would have very little chance of becoming a leading school of law if the University closed won the day.

Still, despite the Muller sale and the wrenching cost cutting and the firing of scores of people, the financial condition of the University remained precarious. It became clear to Sawhill that the only way to really save the University was through fundraising. Until that time fundraising was minimal; the Board did not view fundraising as a priority and faculty and deans were only minimally involved in raising funds from private sources.

Fundraising: Everybody's Job: Rule I

Sawhill, on the other hand knew that fundraising had to become a priority of the *whole University*, including its President, its Chairman, its Board, its Deans, and its Faculty if it was to survive. Fundraising, he said frequently, cannot be left only to the development staff. It cannot be assigned only to a staff of fundraisers. It must be viewed as central, pivotal to the organization's life. It must be viewed as a priority of every component within the institution. Many times executive directors of nonprofit organizations, including presidents of universities believe that if they have a strong development staff, they can distance themselves from the fundraising effort. If the leadership of your organizations thinks that way, your fundraising efforts are doomed. Every unit in your organization must be involved or you cannot succeed.

Many organizations view their fundraisers moreover as the least important component in their organization. As a result, fundraisers are not always treated with professional respect and do not receive the salaries they deserve. No organization can treat their fundraisers in that fashion and be successful in its efforts to raise money. There are 1.8 million nonprofit organizations in the United States today. They raised, in 2007, $306 billion. In achieving that remarkable goal, fundraisers played a key role. It must be kept in mind that without a flourishing nonprofit sector, our country would not be what it is today. And without the fundraisers, the nonprofit organizations would have difficulty surviving. It's this philosophy that John Sawhill projected very dramatically to the University as a whole. He faced a Board that was not respectful of its fundraisers, and did not have a culture of giving. The two factors are usually different sides of the same coin and he made clear that both sides must change.

The Role of the President: Rule II

As the President, he set the example. He increased salaries for the development staff. He put the office of Senior Vice President for External Affairs next to his. He would meet with the Senior Vice President and other development staff throughout each week to go over the week's fundraising activities. He insisted that the development staff arrange at least a minimum of four to five fundraising meetings a week for him—not an easy task. He constantly stated that "good fundraising is not achieved by postage stamps, but by shoe leather." In this he meant that only meetings and more meetings and more meetings—to meet people at lunches, breakfasts, and dinners—could identify donors. Only in this way could he tell the NYU story and begin the cultivation of donors—a prerequisite to effective fundraising. "That is why," he said, "the process is called *development, not fundraising.*" He made this clear at every opportunity.

He was a very difficult and hard task master. It was not easy to work with him, but the staff had great respect for his drive and commitment to fundraising. And we knew his approach was correct. Whatever pressure he put upon us, he put on himself too. He never stopped, and he spent probably more than one third of his time in fundraising. But he felt that only in that way would he be able to save the University. In short, he set the tone within the NYU academic community concerning fundraising. He made it clear that he would be the principal salesman, that he would make calls himself, but that he expected to get help from every unit within the University. This intense Presidential involvement in fundraising was carried on by his successors Dr. John Brademas, Dr. L. Jay Oliva, and by the current NYU President, John Sexton. It is no exaggeration to say that John Sexton is probably one of the best fundraisers in the academic world today.

Dr. Oliva, before he was President, was Vice President for Academic Affairs under John Sawhill and Provost under John Brademas. In both capacities he was responsible for the academic directions of the University, around which the fundraising developed. The University could not raise money unless it had an academic vision that excited donors. Dr. Oliva was a key player in developing that vision. John Brademas and John

24

Sexton continued that role. Dr. Brademas, in addition, was deeply involved in projecting "the image" of NYU to the media. He understood the important connection between fundraising and visibility. He was a master of public relations.

Later this Case Study examines the importance of having "a unique vision" and the role of public relations in fundraising. Suffice to say here that both are essential in effective fundraising and the President or CEO of a nonprofit must play a role in both areas. NYU has been fortunate in having Presidents in the last 35 years that understood that.

John Sawhill also explained repeatedly that when people gave a gift, they want to meet the head of the organization, the man who is running the organization, the person who is going to care for their money. And that is why he, as the President, had to play so intimate a role in the fundraising. People who gave money wanted to meet the CEO; they want to be sure that they can trust him and that their money would be spent well. That was his basic philosophy; that was what he preached at every opportunity that he had.

He also made clear to the faculty and deans that he couldn't raise money in a vacuum. They had to give him ideas, they had to be concerned with fundraising in the same way that he was. Faculty, therefore, were encouraged to come up with ideas that he could then package and promote. Faculty, understanding the dire needs of the University, were only too glad to help. And their efforts were rewarded in the saving of the University.

The Chairman of the Board of Trustees: Rule III

Sawhill recognized too that he could not do fundraising alone, even with the help of a well run development office. He required a Chairman of the Board committed to fundraising and for whom fundraising was his priority. His first step, therefore, on assuming the Presidency, was to find someone who would chair the Board, who would work with him closely in fundraising, and would have contacts within the city of New York that could help with finding prospective donors.

Finding an effective Chairman is probably one of the most important functions of a CEO or President. This applies whether the organization is a large one or a small one. The Chairman is absolutely critical. The President or CEO should not rush in this task. He or she should be prepared to spend a good deal of time in this search. Sawhill followed that rule. He took his time and he chose very wisely. The person he recommended as the new Chairman of the Board was Laurence Tisch, who was Co-Chair and CEO of the Loews Corporation and CEO of CAN Financial Services. His companies owned real estate, hotels, movies, insurance, Bulova Watch Co., and Lorillard Tobacco. He graduated from NYU in 1942. Mr. Tisch had also been involved in many philanthropic ventures in the city. He was highly respected, a very successful businessman, a generous philanthropist himself, and someone who understood the dynamics involved in an effective fundraising campaign. He knew the New York City philanthropic community and it, in turn, knew and admired him.

The Board of Trustees: Rule IV

Tisch together with Sawhill made clear to the Board that they expected Board members not merely to sit on the Board because it was an honor and privilege. Board members had serious responsibilities. They must attend meetings; they must serve on committees; they must participate in budget and audit discussions and in the decisions involving the academic mission of the University. And they would be expected to give money, to help get money, or, to put it crassly, get off the Board.

Obviously just being able to fulfill those functions and to make a gift were not the sole requirements for sitting on the Board. Board members had to be persons concerned with social issues and particularly with education, and the community had to view them as decent and honest people.

On a related note, it is an axiom in fundraising that "people give to people." Donors are going to give to someone they know, some peer, somebody involved in their life in some fashion, somebody whom they respect. Again, that makes the role of the Trustees so important. They know prospective donors. They must open the doors for the President and Chairman to meet them. They have to be prepared to go out with the President or the Chairman or the Directors of Development on such calls. Over and over again Tisch and Sawhill reiterated their mantra: no organizations, large or small, can afford to have people on its Board who are not ready to give money and help raise it.

Some members of the Board accepted this new "culture of giving;" some left the board; and new members were added.

Both Sawhill and Tisch believed that donors to New York University would come from "the fire group," i.e. finance, insurance, and real estate. Those were the industries of New York City. Those were the industries in which many NYU alumni were involved, and, therefore would be most receptive to requests from the University. With this in mind they added to the Board several leading realtors, Presidents of two major banks, the Chairman of Bear Sterns, plus an important representative of Lehman Brothers; two leading figures from the insurance world, at AIG and Metropolitan Life. It was probably, when completed during Brademas's and Oliva's time, the most impressive Board in the city of New York. It continues, under John Sexton, the current President, to be that kind of Board.

Development Committee: The Use of Volunteers: Rule V

George Heyman, a Managing Director of Lehman Brothers, with a distinguished career in the financial and philanthropic world, was chosen to head a Trustee Development Committee, which consisted of a small group of trustees that were responsible for the overall campaign. This committee met frequently and in between meetings was kept informed by Mr. Heyman and by the development staff on the phone or in memos, about meetings, success stories, failures, new prospects and dollars received. They were indispensable in directing the campaign, and in suggesting new donors and taking special assignments.

Having a small group that is assigned the special task of working exclusively on development is an important component in any campaign. It provides, moreover, another vehicle for volunteers, which are important in the functioning of an organiza-

25

121

tion—and especially important in fundraising. Every study shows that people who volunteer generally give more money than those who do not. It gives the volunteers, moreover, something to do. Most volunteers complain that they are not used effectively by their organization. They attend meetings, and sometimes make a gift. For most people those are not satisfactory functions; they want more. Fundraising is an answer to that problem. It provides many important functions for volunteers, including working on special events, on phonathons, working on fundraising dinners, finding new donors, making calls, writing letters, and participating in stewardship.

Development Office Staff: Centralized: Well Paid and Respected: Rule VI

Sawhill paid a great deal of attention to the development staff and how it was organized. He found a University in which all of the different schools had their own fundraising goals and their own staff and acted as if they were independent organizations. John Sawhill developed a centralized fundraising operation. There was one goal for the entire University with each school having to raise a specific portion of this goal. Each of the schools' fundraising staff was to be *hired, fired, and supervised* by the Senior Vice President for External Affairs, who reported to the President. But, even with this centralization, each Dean was expected to be part of the "team" and play an important role in the fundraising in his or her school.

Deans generally were involved in raising smaller gifts, $500,000 or less, plus alumni cultivation. The larger gifts were usually assigned to the President or a trustee.

The Senior Vice President was to act as the "clearing house" regarding donors, and to coordinate the schools' solicitations so that duplication in requests was avoided. If a Dean wanted to visit Mr. Smith, for example, but another school had been cultivating Mr. Smith in the past, it was the job of the Senior Vice President to act as the referee, to decide which school had priority and if he or she sensed a conflict, the President, who was the final arbitrator, was consulted.

The organization of the development office was simple.

A Senior Vice President for External Affairs, whose portfolio included fundraising and alumni affairs, was in charge of the development office. The staff included:

- The Director of Development who supervised the entire staff, also serviced the Senior Vice president, George Heyman, and the Trustee Development Committee. The Director had one major gift officer working with him. Both reported directly to the Senior Vice President.

- Each school had a school Development Director plus anywhere from one to 10 other development staff. Law and Medicine had the largest number of staff as they had the largest goals. The other schools either shared a Development Officer or had, at most, two to three development officers.

- One person was hired for coordinating the work with founda-

tions and one person to do the same for corporations.
- One person was assigned to planned giving.

- One person was responsible for special events. He had one assistant.

- Several people were hired to work on alumni.

- Several people were assigned to a Research Center and a special computer system was established to track gifts, do research as to possible donors, and permit follow up and stewardship.

- Three writers were also on staff to help do "thank you" letters and proposals.

- In addition every development staff member was expected to write their own "thank you" letters, do drafts of proposals, etc.

- There was a support staff of about ten secretaries.

It was, by today's standards, a very small staff. As the fundraising grew, year by year, it was increased modestly. It never was very large.

Choose Development People Who Are Interesting Human Beings: Rule VII

While education and experience are important in choosing development staff, the development staff at NYU was supposed to have, in addition, an entrepreneurial spirit, and be creative, able to write, speak, and relate to people. Regardless of the position they held within the development office, staff had to be "interesting, well-read people"—so that donors would enjoy talking and relating to them. For fundraising is not primarily "asking people for money." That's part of it, but not all. It's *cultivation of people*. It's developing relationships.

Here is where "the art," not the science, comes in. Here is where your personality and how you relate to people are key. And here is where every situation is different—as different as every donor.

By adulthood, much of a person's personality is set. But there are ways to change it—to improve. Of course, read the *Chronicle of Philanthropy* and other books and magazines on development and philanthropy. But more important, read the *New York Times, The Wall Street Journal, The Economist, The New Yorker* and other magazines; read books; read novels, biographies, history and join organizations; become a whole person; be interested in the society in which you live; show that you are interested in current issues—in politics, in education, healthcare, the environment, women's rights, etc. This makes it possible to cultivate a donor by discussing areas of his or her interest. When Mr. Tisch was involved with CBS, the staff that related to him was asked to read everything that the press was reporting about CBS. Why were people critical of Mr. Tisch? What was happening in his news division? Why is *Murphy Brown* a success? What happened to *Murder She Wrote?* Development staff was urged to read those articles so that they could talk to Mr. Tisch in the area of his greatest interest. Developing a relationship starts with such conversations.

Understand Why People Give: Rule VIII

Everyone involved in fundraising should understand why people give. The reasons are many and often complex.

- Altruism: Many people give because they believe in a cause that they hope will make the world better.

- Give Back: The desire to repay an organization, a school, often a hospital, for helping them—is a strong motivation for giving. Hospital campaigns are often based on "grateful patients" who want to give something back to the doctor who helped them. Alumni campaigns also depend on this emotion.

- Who Asks: People are prone to give to people they know, trust, and respect. It is harder to say "no" to a friend or business associate than to a stranger. For that reason it is important to choose wisely as to who will join you on a call. "People give to People" is not merely a catch phrase but a valuable bit of advice.

- To Be a Part of a Social Group: In every community there is usually a special social group or groups, that people want to be a part of. Sometimes it represents the "socially and economically elite" i.e. the New York Met Opera or the Met Museum of Art in NYC. People will frequently give a donation just to be seen with this group. It's "the place to be." Other people find a sense of belonging when they are part of a group and make this gift to be assured of their place in this group.

- Tax Benefits: American tax laws are generous in providing tax benefits for charitable gifts. Although such benefits may be one factor in making such gifts—it is not the most important. Moreover many large gifts were given to charities long before the Tax Code added its tax incentives. (The Rockefeller and Carnegie gifts are just two examples.)

- Being Asked: Don't underestimate the importance of "asking." Many times people don't give simply because no one asked. And never be ashamed of asking. You are asking for a good cause—not for yourself. And keep in mind that people are often flattered that they are asked.

- Feel Good: Strange as it may seem, many people just "feel good" when they make a gift. There is a warm, often indescribable feeling of pleasure when one can help another person or a cause.

- Self Interest: Some people give because they believe there is a benefit in business or socially from the gift. This is especially true of corporations.

- Religious Commitment: All major religions include a mandate to care for the poor, the aged, and the orphan and to help "your brother in need." All studies show that religious affiliation influences giving.

Be Able to Verbalize the Uniqueness of Your Product: Rule IX

While the President was recruiting a new Chairman and new Board members, he was also working with appropriate staff and faculty to define what was special and unique about NYU. As said before, there are 1.8 million nonprofits in New York City. Why should donors give to NYU? Why is NYU special? Why is it unique? These are basic questions that every organization must ask itself when it begins a fundraising campaign.

NYU started from the assumption that its biggest competitors were the CUNY open enrollment colleges, and Columbia. As for the CUNY schools, NYU decided that it had to distinguish itself dramatically from those schools. It had to cut back on its size, raise its SAT requirements, raise its academic standards, consolidate its operations on the square, build its College of Arts and Science, use its fundraising to attract distinguished faculty, and present itself not as a "last resort university" or an open enrollment university—open to everyone—but rather an academically demanding university that would recruit top students, and top faculty. More than half of the money raised in its opening campaign was devoted to attracting new faculty and in providing scholarships for top students.

As for Columbia, NYU distinguished itself in a very special fashion. It described Columbia as a school with a wall around it, divorced from New York City; a special enclave of privilege in upper Manhattan. NYU on the other hand had no wall around it, it was part and parcel of the city of New York. It would become a "private university in the public service." Every one of our schools was asked to develop programs with New York City institutions. For example, our school of education developed scores of programs with the public schools of the city. Our Law School developed programs to handle the legal problems of the poor in the City. Our Medical School developed an increasing number of programs with Bellevue. Our Dental School sent out vans to nursing homes in the city to treat the aged who had dental problems. Our Tisch School of the Arts developed very close relations with the theaters in the city. And our business school developed programs together with Wall Street and the financial world. So when you attended NYU you not only received an education academically, but you were also exposed to the real world, to New York City, with its myriad of institutions, businesses, professionals, and the performing and visual arts. Thurs New York City would become the campus of NYU!

As part of its transformation NYU decided to do extensive recruitment outside of New York City. No longer would it be a subway school (like the CUNY colleges). Instead it would be a national and international university. This required using some of the money that was raised not only for scholarships and faculty, but also for building dormitories and other facilities for a "living on campus" experience. (Very little was put in the endowment, as the trustees decided first to "build" the University and only when that was completed, to set aside funds

27

123

for endowment.) Seven new residence halls were built, offering modern suites with kitchens, living rooms, cable TV, all wired for Internet connections. One of the most impressive dormitories was the Palladium building, which houses 973 students, encompasses a 65,000 square foot athletic and recreation facility that includes a pool for swimming, diving, water polo, a basketball court, and exercise space.

In addition, a new sports center was built, providing facilities for basketball, tennis, swimming, fencing, volleyball, and dance. A new student center, with extensive facilities for student clubs was built. It is a signature building on Washington Square and holds a 1,022 seat state-of-the-art theater—the largest theater south of 42nd street and the only performing center south of Lincoln Center. Its projection booth and integrated audio equipment enables it to hold film screenings and film festivals, including the TSOA first run film festival and the bi-annual NYU international student film festival. As a result, our connections with Broadway expanded and in the performing arts and in filmmaking studies NYU is now the number one university in the country.

All of these facilities, that cost more than $1 billion, plus the new classrooms and laboratories gave a new face to the University. More than 11,000 students now live on campus at NYU. We are dramatically different from the CUNY colleges. And our deep involvement with New York City differentiates us dramatically from Columbia.

It has given us a unique face, something that has been critical in our fundraising.

So, whether you are a university, a large organization or a small one, it is a basic rule of effective fundraising that you try to present your "product" in a way that makes it unique and special.

Process in Place: Rule X

Now we come to the most difficult part of a fundraising campaign, i.e., to develop a process that will bring in a maximum number of donors.

Eighty-three percent of the money raised by NYU came from gifts of $1 million or more. This is not unique to NYU. It is true of any major campaign. What a major gift is will depend very much on the size and budget of the organization involved. It could be as small as $500 and as large as $10 million or more. But whatever the size of the major gift, it is critical to any campaign, large or small. [On page 31 under Alumni and Annual Campaigns, we discuss other aspects of fundraising. In this section on process we will concentrate on major gifts through individual solicitations.]

Now back to the process. While many organizations may develop modifications of this process, we are listing below the steps that NYU took and takes in developing its campaign.

1. The President of the University, having made fundraising an all university priority and having put a chairman in place plus a Board understanding its fundraising responsibilities, now begins his campaign by asking the chairman of the Board for his gift.

2. After the Chairman made his gift, which should be viewed as a "lead" gift, he and the President choose a few potential donors among the trustees, who they felt were capable of a large gift and with whom they had good working relationships. They then visited those trustees, all of whom made their gifts of $1 million or more to start the campaign.

3. After these preliminary gifts were made, a note went out to every trustee telling them that a campaign was beginning. No public announcement would be made until we had visited every trustee and some potential donors so that we had some idea of how much money we could expect in the campaign.

4. After this letter went out, the senior vice president in charge of development, the president, the chairman of the board, and sometimes other trustees visited every single other trustee. In most cases they were not asked for money at this time. Instead, they were told about the campaign and the University's needs. They were asked if they would give us a list of any friends or potential donors who we could put in our database.

We also asked them if they would "help us" in the campaign. We were deliberately vague at this point, merely trying to discover whether they would be prepared to make some gift once the campaign began. In some cases an "ask" was made, but this depended on individual circumstances.

5. After this visit, the development staff began to work together with the research center. Other names were collected from our alumni lists, donor lists, etc. and a huge database was put together that would be the foundation of our campaign.

6. The University then had some idea of what its potential fundraising goals could be. Some organizations hire consultants to do this—a feasibility study. NYU never did that. It believed that its staff was capable of putting this together. The University was not prepared to pay $100,000 or more that consultants charge for this study. Moreover, if our own staff was involved in assembling the database, they would have a better feel for the potential that the University had in raising its funds.

7. As stated above, we started with our trustees. We found out everything we could about them; their ability to give; what their interests were; and what charitable gifts they had recently made. The people in research were indispensable in collecting this information. We then brought these names to our Trustee Development Committee.

8. We went over these names with the Trustee Development Committee not only to get their opinion about the prospects, but to get their comments about who should be meeting with each of the prospects—assuming we were planning to go further with them. For example, if the person was in real estate, we would discuss what real estate per-

son should meet with him. If he was in insurance or finance, we would think of people who we felt were his peers and someone that he would respect. During the 20 years that Mr. Tisch was chairman, he joined most of these meetings—as did the president and the senior vice president for external affairs. They had as many as four or five meetings a week until every trustee was personally visited.

9. After we identified the person who we thought might want to support a particular project and identified the person who should be the one to go to the first meeting, the staff in development usually called that potential donor on behalf of Mr. Tisch and the president and asked for an appointment. We usually explained on the phone that we wanted to bring the person up to date on NYU and ask their advice on something in which the University was interested. If, for example, we were going to meet a man interested in investments, we made certain to comment about our investment policy, explaining at breakfast that we hoped he could help us as we explored this area.

10. We usually had our meetings at breakfast. This was convenient to the businessmen. (At that time, and this shall be commented on later, we did not have as many women on our prospect list as we would have today.) At these breakfasts we did not say: "We are glad to meet you and could you give us money?" We never did that. At those meetings we talked about their interests, a little about the world, areas of mutual interests and then, if appropriate, we would ask his advice on some University policy. We would then discuss particular programs at the University in which we thought they might be interested. And we listened and let the prospect talk—so that we would discover their special interests. Then we asked whether they would have any time to take a tour of the University, have lunch with the President, and get a better sense of what we were doing. We tried to get a date at breakfast for such a follow up meeting. If they accepted our request for a visit, we knew they were interested.

11. When they came down to the Square and had lunch with the President, and an appropriate Dean and faculty from areas in which we thought they might be interested, we took them to visit those areas. At this luncheon with the President and Dean we also tried to involve them in something. If there was going to be a concert or film festival at Tisch, we would invite them to that. If there was a seminar at the Law School, we would invite them to that. If we had an advisory committee on filmmaking, we would, if appropriate, invite them to sit on that committee. The purpose of these meetings was to try to involve them in some aspect of University activity. Involvement is key: it is the most effective way of developing a relationship. Every organization should try to have their donors visit their offices. Seeing a program at work is worth a hundred words.

12. We did not rush to ask for money. The quicker you ask, the less money you will receive. We were very careful to develop a relationship with the prospective donor before we would ask for money

13. Once we received the commitments of the trustees, we continued the process we used with our trustees of finding new prospects through research and suggestions from our trustees; doing our homework on each prospect; holding lunches, breakfasts, etc.; and cultivating each prospective donor and involving them in some fashion in the University. It is a slow process. There are no shortcuts.

14. While this is going on, the President was meeting with each dean to determine their needs. When we had a respectable amount of money in hand or pledged, and had a good idea of what was needed in the University, a proposed goal and plan for the campaign was brought to the Board of Trustees. Once they approved it, we then went public.

15. Our public announcement usually came at a luncheon. The President and Chairman of the Board would speak; goals were set; the lead gifts were announced; and a campaign committee was created. This was usually the Trustee Development Committee with a few additional trustees and donors added.

We made the announcement as exciting as we could, trying to find something in our goals that would interest the media. For example, if some of the money would be used for some research in malaria, we would feature it. If we planned a new dorm, we would have pictures, etc. In short, announcing a campaign is as much or more a PR event as a fundraising event.

16. In designing your campaign and your list of prospective donors, do not forget the women. They not only should be on your board, but they should be intimately involved in the committees of your organization. Women today own 51.3% of the nation's wealth. They own the majority of all stocks traded on the NYSE. Many have inherited their wealth (women live 7–10 years longer than men) and many are now earning very good salaries. Many have important positions in law firms, in the medical profession, and on Wall Street.

Should fundraisers have a different approach when they are soliciting women than when they are soliciting men? There is no unanimity about this. My own experience has been that there are not many fundamental differences. The differences are usually age and economic status—not gender. But more research is clearly needed. I believe that when you have a good product and you sell it with passion and commitment and you know the woman is interested in such projects, and the right person has come to meet with her, there are no gender differences in the way that you sell your product.

17. Be certain in your campaign to pay attention to planned giving. One-third of gifts made by individuals come through wills, charitable lead trusts, pooled income, etc. This is a very important area and no campaign should be without someone in charge of this. That person should be a lawyer. In addition to the person assigned to planned giving, every member of the staff should know about this area. They should take courses; read books that are devoted to planned giving; and be able to at least begin preliminary conversations about these instruments with potential donors. Usually the staff person does not have to go into great detail. It is appropriate for him or her to say: "If you are interested in this as a method of giving a gift to NYU, may I suggest that you talk with your lawyer and your accountant." That is probably the best way to go. But knowledge about planned giving is critical.

18. In putting together a database and planning your campaign, using the Internet and technology is absolutely essential. The research people have now at their disposal technological systems that segment people. They have research tools that can give them an enormous amount of information, including Hoovers.com, Edgar.com, the Foundation Center, Guidstar.org and Grantsmart.org. Your staff should also read the *New York Times, Forbes, Business Week*, the *Economist*, the *Wall Street Journal*, and other publications that relate to business. You can get a good deal of information from these sources as well as the many sources on the Internet today.

19. Never forget stewardship—caring for the donor after he makes his gift. A donor who has already made a gift is your best prospect for future gifts. Keep him or her informed on what is happening with the project he has funded. Send them regularly information about your organization and remember birthdays or special times in a donor's life and constantly think of ways to keep the donor involved. Accountability and disclosure are key words you must never forget. And, for major donors, always find the time for a visit and a phone call.

Capital Campaign: Know What It Is and When to Embark On It: Rule XI

Everything discussed in the preceding section on process is preliminary to launching a capital campaign. The principal components of a capital campaign are: it is intense; it runs for a *specific period* of time; and has a *specific purpose or purposes.*

Following the NYU model, you do not begin a capital campaign until you have a good chairman in place; you have a board ready to help in fundraising; you made fundraising an organizational priority; you have a good development staff; you received some major gifts from some of your trustees and other potential donors; and you develop a large enough donor base of possible future donors that would assure the success of the campaign. You also must make certain before you go public that you know what your priorities are.

Only when New York University had all of those components in place did John Sawhill announce a capital campaign in 1976. The campaign would be for three years and attempt to raise $111 million. The goals were to increase scholarship funds, to continue its extensive recruitment of top faculty, and move ahead with its building program.

Building an endowment was not part of the goals of this campaign. The trustees were very clear in stating that first the University must regain its position as a major educational institution. It had to put the money it raised in paying its debts, getting top students and top faculty, and continuing to build the facilities to accommodate those groups.

The campaign, as I said above, was for three years. That meant that only $37 million would have to be raised each year. Since the University was already raising close to $30 million at that time, setting a $37 million goal was not exorbitant. The importance was that it was the first campaign the University had launched in a long time. People understood the need for it. The fear of bankruptcy was still hanging over the University and getting private money remained a high priority.

One word about setting your goals. Do not set them too high. It is better to be modest and surpass your goal than to set a goal that you cannot reach. Once the goals were set and everything else was in place, the University held a luncheon at a hotel in the city to make its announcement. Its lead gifts were reported. Special praise was given to those who helped through those gifts to start the campaign. The President and Chairman of the Board spoke. It had the aura of an exciting event. The press covered it and the University was off with flying colors to the first of its many campaigns.

Such capital campaigns provide special opportunity for new brochures, for providing medals and citations for major donors, and provide many opportunities for the use of volunteers.

At the end of three years, NYU surpassed its goal and was prepared in 1982 to announce another campaign—this one to raise "a million a week for 100 weeks." That was a catchy phrase that caught the attention not only of the potential donors and trustees, but of the press. Actually when translated into yearly figures the "one million a week" meant the University would have to raise $52 million a year. That was not an exorbitant number, as we had proved that we were able to raise $35–37 million in each of the preceding three years. Again, we were cautious in setting our goal. We knew what we could raise. We were not extravagant in choosing a million a week for two years. But the idea of raising that much money each week was a very exciting vision and it helped generate a sense of importance, urgency, and excitement within the University.

The "One-Million a Week for 100 Weeks Campaign" was again a huge success. The University raised $110 million by 1984. And in 1985 it then felt confident enough to announce-ment a "One-Billion Dollar" capital campaign to be raised in 15 years. It was one of the first universities in the country to set a goal of one billion dollars. That meant that the University would now have to raise $70 million a year. Keep in mind that again that was not an exorbitant amount, since we already proved we could raise $52 million a year. But the "One-Billion Dollar" number attracted the press (something all capital campaigns aim for) and it excited the leadership by the audacity of the number "one billion." This campaign too was more successful, raising its goal in 10 years, not 15.

It was during this capital campaign that the University created the Sir Harold Acton Society. All donors who contributed one million dollars or more got a beautiful Sir Harold Acton Medal at a black-tie dinner. To this day, once a year the University holds a Sir Harold Acton Gala Dinner. It serves as an incentive for million-dollar and over gifts and it added an exciting tone to the campaign.

Today NYU is completing its third billion dollar campaign, having completed a $2.5 billion campaign on time and raising more than $3.1 billion. This is attributed to the exceptional fundraising skills of President Sexton and Senior Vice President LaMorte.

Do Not Forget Your Annual Campaign: Rule XII

So far in this case study we have concentrated on major gifts and "one-on-one" solicitations. But no campaign should ever forget or ignore the small gifts that one can count on year after year in response to an annual campaign drive. These gifts are important because they are usually unrestricted, which is very important for an organization to have and because, from their ranks often come future larger gifts. Annual appeals usually involve direct mail, i.e., appeal letters, followed by telephone calls (phonathon or a telemarketing company) and if research shows that the annual gift a donor makes indicates a potential for a larger gift, then meetings and cultivation follow.

Usually current donors who gave in the last appeal are written to first. But donors who gave previously but not yet in this campaign and persons who never gave but have some relationship to the organization are also sent solicitation letters as the campaign unfolds. The secret of direct mail is, of course, the letter and even the envelope. It must tell the organizational story in an exciting way. It cannot be too long. It is a difficult piece to write and many times requires special help. Organizations have become more sophisticated these days with the computers help in segmenting their lists by age, occupation, gender, location, etc., in order to better tailor their direct mail appeals. This should be done whenever possible.

The phone calls that follow can be made by a telemarketing company or by volunteers or by both. NYU has always used paid NYU students to make these calls. There is something especially appealing when students make the calls. But working with students and volunteers is often difficult. They need more training and are not always reliable. For that reason many nonprofit organizations use a telemarketing company. Their professionals need less training and are more sophisticated callers, who generally always show up. But they do not have the special appeal that the volunteer and/or the student has. I think every organization must examine this themselves and decide which is more effective for them. Sometimes a combination of both is the best.

Be certain that in negotiations with your telemarketing company you are clear about how much money the company keeps and how much money they return to you. On page 8 of this book is an article that discusses this problem and indicates the large amount of money that some companies keep — as much as 75%! The Better Business Bureau suggests no more than 35%.

Annual appeals should not stop during a capital campaign. Donors should be told early in the campaign the need for the unrestricted annual gift and why their gift to the capital campaign should be viewed as "over and above" their annual gift. And while this is the general wisdom often given on this subject, it is more complicated. To some it might seem in bad taste to ask a donor who just gave a million dollar gift to the capital campaign to give another $1,000 to the annual fund. The donor might feel he is being "nickled and dimed." In other cases he would understand the difference between the two campaigns and be quite willing to make this added donation. In short, each donor should be handled separately and no blanket rule should apply. Here timing is most important too. Try not to make your direct mail appeal at the same time a donor is being visited for a major gift. Again, each donor must be handled separately.

Special Events—Part of a Fundraising Campaign: Rule XIII

The number and type of special events are limitless and can include luncheons, dinners, galas, golf and tennis outings, theater parties, auctions, fashion shows, etc. It was the opinion of the staff at New York University that most special events, especially dinners and galas, were not cost effective and did not raise large sums of money. For example, if an organization sold 500 tickets at $1,000 each, it would gross $500,000. In today's market it would cost at least $250,000 for the food, hotel costs, flowers, liquor, invitations, program, etc., netting only $250,000. The latter figure, moreover, does not include staff time in making hundreds of calls to get 500 people to buy tickets. And the details in any dinner or gala are enormous and also require a great deal of staff time. If, however, the event is used as a way of soliciting gifts prior to the dinner, or if the dinner is sponsored by an organization or person, then it might be viewed as worth the amount of time, effort and costs involved.

But there is another function in having dinners and other special events. Dinners have a valuable public relations component. If the program and the speakers are well chosen then the chance of getting an item in the press is very real. Many organizations use their dinners and galas for that kind of public visibility. Galas also bring in new people. If you are going to honor someone, he or she will unquestionably bring in their friends and that gives you additional names for your database. So do not get me wrong, there are advantages in holding such special events, but I do not view them as a way of raising a great deal of money. I view them more as a public relations event, getting more visibility and bringing in some new people for future development and cultivation.

Never Forget Public Relations: Rule XIV

Do not underestimate the importance of public relations. Media coverage and other public relations techniques not only for dinners, but for all aspects of organizational work is an important prerequisite to any effective campaign. Your organization's work,

31

its contributions to the community, its leadership, must be known before people will make a gift.

Every effort must be made to get your stories to the press, radio, or TV. Do not concentrate on the *New York Times* and the *Wall Street Journal*. Local press and local radio stations are eager for stories. Cultivate members of the press as you would prospects. Send them invitations to events. Send them ideas you may have about a possible story. Send them material about the programs you are involved in. If new or interesting members join your board, try to get stories about them or profiles in the newspapers. Write your press releases carefully because many press officers are so busy that they will use a press release exactly the way it is sent to them. If your release is well written, this encourages them to use your release.

You annual report and any program materials should be widely distributed. The story headlined in the *New York Times* shown below did more for the reputation of New York University than any fundraising activity we could have ever conceived.

Technology is very much related to how your image is projected. How you appear on the Web is critical. At NYU we consider our website as the public face of our University. We have hundreds of professors on the Web describing themselves and their courses. We have pictures of our dormitories, our labs, and our sports center, etc. You can and must do the same with your organization. This is especially important for younger people.

Make Certain to Have a Program in Place for Corporation and Foundation Proposal Solicitations: Rule XV

In 2007 foundations gave $38.5 billion, which was 12.6% of total gifts made to charity in that year. In spite of the fact that this is a relatively small amount in relationship to the 83% that came from individuals, it is very important in the fundraising life of your organization. When a foundation gives you a grant it signifies that a group of very knowledgeable people in a peer review process approved your organization and the project you want funded. It is like a Good Housekeeping seal of approval. This inspires other donors to do the same.

Today there are approximately 70,000 foundations throughout the country. About 30,000 are small family foundations. They must give away 5% of their assets each year. Some staff person in your organization must be responsible for foundations—studying their annual reports; what they support; whom they support; and what their guidelines say. Your organization must know the answers to these questions as they relate to many of the foundations that you believe would be willing to support you. You must look at their guidelines. You must try wherever possible to match their interests with yours. All of this information is accessible to the public through the Foundation Center. And, of course, every foundation issues an important annual report which lists the gifts that it made; the organizations it contributes to; and what guidelines it uses in making gifts.

At NYU we would also try to have the president meet the head of some of the major foundations – not to ask for money, but to get acquainted. If you are not in a position to meet with the President, you can meet with program directors and get

acquainted with them. At such meetings you do not necessarily ask for money. You can just get acquainted and let them meet you and know about the organization that you represent. That always helps. Keep in mind that foundations are looking for creative, innovative programs that can be easily evaluated. They do not fund endowment or organizational expenses. They fund projects and programs.

In planning your solicitation of a foundation, sometimes a phone call to the program officer will help. In some cases a letter of inquiry should be the first step. That letter should indicate the project you have in mind; why you think your organization is qualified to conduct it; what it would cost—the budget; and your desire to meet with someone at the foundation to discuss it. If the response is positive, you then either meet with someone at the foundation or prepare a bigger proposal. These proposals should not be 50-page dissertations. They should be brief and should explain succinctly what it is you want funded; why you think you are qualified to handle the project; why you believe it is unique; and again, how you plan to evaluate it. If you can get a meeting, of course, that is the best way to proceed. If not, you have to rely upon the proposals that you send in writing.

Corporations do not give as much as foundations, but they are another important source of income. In 2007 they gave $15.6 billion, which was 5.1% of the giving for that year. They give either cash, services, and many times equipment and products. Some give directly from the corporation itself and some set up foundations. Corporations give for many reasons: some want to be good citizens; others give because it is good for their business. Some give for both reasons. Some economists, like Milton Friedman of the University of Chicago, believe that corporations exist solely to make money for their stockholders. Others believe that corporations have a social responsibility to their community and to their country as well. Most corporations in the United States follow this latter path and do assume, to some degree, their corporate social responsibility. But I have no doubt they also are motivated by the fact that it is good for their business.

There are about 15,000 public corporations in the United States. Information about them is filed with the Securities and Exchange Commission and the Internet will provide you with that information. Each of them also put out annual reports, which again will give you a great deal of information about their interests and their charitable giving. Here, like with the foundations, it is important to keep your proposals short, succinct and well written. It is best to go to those corporations that do business in your community. Most corporations like to make their charitable gift where they are located. If a bank has a branch in your area, it is more likely that branch will contribute to you than to some organization in another community. Keep this in mind when you decide on which companies to approach.

Understanding How and Whom to "Ask:" Rule XVI

The "Ask" is probably the most important part of any fundraiser's responsibility. It requires careful preparation, thorough knowledge about what the "ask" entails, and as much information as possible about the prospective donor. Most fundraisers, including Presidents, Board members, and volunteers, are very uncomfortable with asking for money. Some of them are absolutely terrified. They would much prefer to write a letter than to have a visit at which they actually have to ask for money. The best approach, I believe, is one that does not "ask for money;" instead, one asks for support for a particular project. Now let me be personal for a moment. While it is difficult or impossible for me to ask for money for myself, it is not difficult to ask for something that I believe is of importance. Always keep this in mind when you are making an ask and keep in mind that a rejection is not a personal rejection, but rather a rejection concerning a project or a program. One cannot take these rejections personally. One has to view them within the context of what fundraising is all about.

To help you feel comfortable about the "ask" and to feel confident in yourself, it is important that you prepare carefully and that you have as much knowledge as possible about the prospective donor and the project you want funded. Some people suggest that you prepare a written script before the meeting and go over it several times, so that you feel comfortable with the approach you will use. This is often a valuable technique.

When exactly the "ask" should be made is hard to answer. Each ask is so different. One has to have a "feel" for when the situation is ready for asking for support. Usually it comes after a period of cultivation. Only the "asker" can ascertain when this should occur.

When a decision has been made to "ask" a quiet place should be chosen. The asker should speak with confidence. Never apologize for asking and let the donor speak. Once you make your request, stop talking. Let the prospective donor respond. How he or she responds will determine what your future strategy should be.

Whether the gift is made or not, be sure to thank the prospective donor, follow up with a letter and/or a call to thank him for his time, and if possible, set another date to discuss the gift further, or to answer questions raised that the asker could not respond to adequately.

Don't give up. Even if the answer is a "no,"—you may have learned something more about the prospect which will help you in further relationships.

Fundraisers Must be Knowledgeable About the Laws that Govern Nonprofits and Be Sensitive to Ethical Issues: Rule XVII

At a time when the media are reporting stories of bad management, board negligence, excess salaries, fraudulent telemarketing, and even criminal behavior in nonprofit organizations, it is imperative that fundraisers be knowledgeable about the laws that govern nonprofits and be especially sensitive to ethical issues involved in fundraising. Since donor trust in nonprofits, moreover, is less than 20% today, it would seem important that such knowledge be part of a fundraiser's qualifications.

More than any other group fundraisers know that trust and donor confidence is critical to any fundraising effort. "If Americans cannot trust their charities," says Mark Everson, IRS Commissioner, at a hearing of the Senate Finance Committee, "they will stop giving and people in need will suffer." And

Senator Charles Grassley, former chairman of the Senate Finance Committee stated: "The charitable community should not stand silently by on the sidelines when the newspapers are filled with flagrant waste and abuse at charity organizations. I am troubled that there is no criticism from the charitable community about the serious problems at American University and the Getty Foundation. Charitable leaders must be a strong voice in condemning inappropriate behavior in their sector."

Such a strong voice can only come about if fundraisers are made sensitive to these issues. Most fundraisers are so busy raising money, meeting their goals, and finding prospects, that rarely do they sit down and consider the ethical issues in what they are doing or even to study the laws that govern their organizations. I urge fundraisers to take courses in these subjects. Such courses are now given at many universities and by many fundraising organizations. It is true that most fundraisers are honest, hardworking, committed, and trustworthy human beings. But even such honest and decent human beings require additional education about their work if they are to continue to be effective. Any hint of subterfuge or abuse or unethical behavior in the fundraising profession surely kills donor generosity. Sensitivity and education can often prevent this. Time should be spent therefore, at development meetings to talk about ethical and legal issues. This is as important in assuring the success of your campaign as the numbers you raise.

One foolish mistake, one act of unethical behavior, can ruin a campaign. The problem at the Red Cross, United Way, Adelphi University, and the Getty Foundation—to mention a few—demonstrate the problems an organization faces when unethical behavior is disclosed.

Of all the rules set forth in this *Case Study*, I consider this rule the most important. If you or your organization is ever viewed as "unethical," "sleazy," "not trustworthy," all the rules set forth in this *Case Study*" are useless. Integrity and trust are the heart and soul of fundraising. Everything else is commentary. ◆

33

Fundraising in Times of Financial Crisis

As to be expected, nonprofit organizations are deeply concerned with the financial crisis. How will it affect fundraising? Will their organization be able to survive? In response to this, the George H. Heyman, Jr. Center for Philanthropy and Fundraising at New York University held several sessions on this critically important subject. This article will summarize the most salient points that came out of these sessions.

First, let me point out that the experts seem to have different points of view concerning the effects of the financial crisis on philanthropy. Some minimize the effects. They quote reports that conclude that in "2007, despite uncertainties in the housing markets and the rising cost of oil, Americans donated more than $306 billion dollars to charity. In the last 40 years the worst one-year decline in inflation adjusted philanthropy was the period 1973–74 during the oil embargo. The decline was 5.4%. If 2007–08 sees an equivalent decline, the total amount of charitable giving in 2008 will be $289.5 billion." This should not be too devastating to bear.

Another report states: "In fact there have been only two periods in the last 40 years with more than a single year absolute decline in giving: the oil embargo of the mid-1970s and after September 11. No other decline has lasted more than a single year. Philanthropy in America is more deeply rooted in culture than in equity share prices."

On the other hand, there is a more negative point of view based on the fact that there are daily reports of massive job lay-offs; a continued severe housing decline; market collapse; consumers not shopping, etc. This point of view believes that this financial crisis is deeper and more severe than in the 1970s. It is closer to the 1930s. Already nonprofits are reporting losses from their larger donors.

I tend to share this more negative concern. I believe we are already in a recession and the nonprofits will surely feel the effect of this economic disaster. How we handle this will clearly effect how our organization will weather this crisis.

Now more specifically: What do we do concerning our fundraising in the face of such a crisis? At our previous sessions, the discussants agreed on the following:

1) First, do not panic. A new President of the United States is taking office with a strong economic stimulus package, which should lessen the fear that is playing a significant role in today's crisis. Fear in itself can be a devastating factor.

2) Whether this recession will be halted by this stimulus package, one does not know. But there are certain things you should and should not do at this point that, I believe, will be helpful whether the recession continues or recedes. These are:

- Do not announce a capital campaign now. Be very cautious. Instead, spend your time meeting privately with every one of your trustees and major donors. Discuss honestly your concerns and your continued needs. Do not be embarrassed to ask whether they have been affected by the market decline. Will this impair their philanthropy? If and when you announce a campaign, will they be in a position to help? And keep in mind while many people are suffering as a result of the crisis, there are others who are not.

- Such an honest discussion of each trustee's or donor's situation might reveal that your situation is not too bad and you will be able to get some major gifts this coming year. These gifts can be part of a "silent campaign" before you go public with an announcement of your capital campaign.

- This feasibility study should, if possible, be conducted by your chief development officer, with your CEO or president and chairman of your board. If this is done "in house," it will give you and your staff a better "feel" for your potential fundraising abilities.

- In meeting with major donors who are hurting, ask whether a readjustment of their pledge would be helpful. If for example, they made a three-year pledge, suggest a five-year payout if that would help.

- Increase your "planned giving program." In times of financial difficulties, some people may find a bequest or a charitable trust or a pooled income gift to be easier to make. Be sure to check tax advantages, as the tax implications will be very important.

- Do not ignore your annual campaign, direct mail, phone solicitations, etc. These represent smaller gifts, which should be easier for donors to make.

- Be sure that your fundraising is as diverse as possible. This means having a program for individual gifts, corporations, and foundations. Big gifts and small gifts are critical. Annual campaigns, as stated above, combined with direct mail and phone solicitations, must be pursued.

- Be sure to use the Internet to its full advantage—both in promoting your organization, in soliciting gifts and as a way for people to make their payments. This is especially useful for younger donors.

- Do not hold expensive events. A "Plaza gala" at a time when people are losing their jobs sends the wrong impression.

- Use your time to have your board examine your programs and projects. Are there programs that can be eliminated? Are you evaluating your programs carefully? Can they be coordinated with other organizations? This is clearly a time to cooperate and coordinate with other organizations working in the same field. Eliminating a program or doing it jointly with another group is not a symbol of defeat; it is a symbol of intelligent planning.

- Examine your staff. Are they being used most effectively? Although you may have to cut your budget, try not to eliminate your fundraisers. They are needed more and more in times of financial crisis. In such times, they are among your most valued staff.

- Be certain to keep your research operation in full gear. It is critical in locating and servicing donors. And like the other development staff, research staff play a very important role in times of crisis.

- Increase the care you give to donors who have made gifts. Call them, write to them, and stay in touch. It is axiomatic that past donors are the best source from whom to get new gifts. Stewardship now becomes more important than ever before.

- Make certain that your board is involved in all of the decisions that you make. Including your budget, decisions to cut, program evaluations, etc.

3) As you can see from the above suggestions, there are no magic bullets. All of your fundraising efforts must continue within the constraints listed above. All of the rules that lay the foundation for effective fundraising must be followed. These rules are:

- Have everyone in your organization, including the president, chairman of the board, and the board, involved in the fundraising. Fundraising is not the sole responsibility of the fundraising staff. It must be everyone's concern.

- Develop relationships with your donors and prospective donors. Such development is critical in fundraising. One-on-one meetings must be set and careful preparation must take place for every meeting.

- Remember that research is critical. You must know as much as you can about every prospective donor before a meeting.

- Major gifts will continue to be at the heart of an effective campaign. Major gifts are raised by shoe leather, not postage stamps. Meetings after meetings must be held with prospects. There is no substitute.

- Again, I repeat: use research and the Internet intelligently. The Internet is especially cost effective.

- Do not ignore your annual campaigns, direct mail, and phonathons. Small gifts are very important. From a small gift a large gift may develop.

- Develop a campaign for soliciting gifts from foundations and corporations.

- Evaluate and examine your programs with an eye to cooperation with other groups and be prepared to eliminate those programs that are least effective.

- Make certain your development staff is respected and well paid. They are critical to your organization's survival.

- And always keep in mind that an important and respected nonprofit that serves an important community function will always find people who will help it survive and grow.

- And keep an optimistic point of view. No one wants to relate to a person who is full of fear. There is an old song called "Smile" that says: "Smile and the world smiles with you. Cry and you cry alone." ◆

Made in the USA
San Bernardino, CA
19 January 2020